Behind the Smile

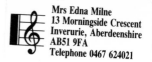
Behind the Smile

My Autobiography

PAUL NICHOLAS
with Douglas Thompson

André Deutsch

Dedication

For Linzi, Mum, Oscar, Susan, Richard, Doug and my kids and everyone who appears in this book except . . . Adolf Hitler.

First published in 1999
by André Deutsch Limited
76 Dean Street
London W1V5HA

www.vci.co.uk

A catalogue record for this book is available from the British Library

ISBN 0 233 99748 2

Typeset by Derek Doyle & Associates, Liverpool
Printed in the UK by MPG Books, Bodmin, Cornwall

Contents

It has always been my experience that you win some and you lose some in this business. What is really important is that you play the game.

– Paul Nicholas, 1999

Never, never ever, put your own money into any production.

– Oscar Beuselinck Sen.

Prologue

Saturday Night at the London Palladium

Here, *this* is dancing, not that Fred Astaire thing – I just move and strut, and *that's dancing!*

– Tony Manero in *Saturday Night Fever*, 1977

I could feel the emotion welling up inside me as the audience began to applaud wildly, cheering and dancing as they looked towards the stage. They were going crazy, clapping their hands in the air and singing along with the music. They were caught up in it. Lost in it. It was magical.

It was 5 May 1999. *Saturday Night Fever* had arrived at the London Palladium. On stage, a young man we had discovered three years earlier was embracing the applause as he belted out the Bee Gees' 'Night Fever'. I was experiencing a heady mix of complete elation and enormous relief. In nearly forty years in showbusiness, I had never been so happy as I was that night. And I wasn't even on stage!

I was sitting in the royal box, watching the first-night performance of *Saturday Night Fever*, a show I had co-produced along with the legendary impresario Robert Stigwood and my partner David Ian. That night I felt so proud of the boy making such a huge success in the lead role of Tony Manero. Adam Garcia had stamped his name and personality on the West End stage version of *Saturday Night Fever* – just as John Travolta had done with the movie.

It was a vindication of the belief we'd had in Adam and the

show. It had involved a lot of tough, exhausting and some-times emotional, rehearsal. If you are going to satisfy an audi-ence, you have to give them quality and value for money. That doesn't just happen; you have to work at it. We had. Our prize was the audience's reaction at the most famous theatre in the world. Knowing we had a hit at the London Palladium was a wonderful bonus.

I first saw the movie of *Saturday Night Fever* when I was living in America in the late 1970s. I knew Robert Stigwood who masterminded the film. A box-office champion since the 1960s, he'd managed the Cream, Eric Clapton and the Bee Gees. He also had his own record label and had produced *Hair*, *Jesus Christ Superstar* and *Evita*. *Saturday Night Fever* was his first major film.

He screened it for me before its release in the large Beverly Hills mansion he was renting from the Hollywood producer Freddie Fields. Fields had just enjoyed a big success with the movie *Looking for Mr Goodbar* starring Diane Keaton. His success was reflected in his home, his swimming pool, his manicured lawns, his palm trees and – most impressively – his own screening room.

I had met John Travolta through Robert and found him a nice, gentle man. He was 23 years old and about to become one of the biggest stars in the world, but he was quite shy. This didn't prepare me for what I was about to see on the screen. I was extremely impressed by his performance. He looked great and acted well but the movie really came alive when he danced to the terrific soundtrack, sung by the Bee Gees. It was electrifying! Bee Gee Barry Gibb later said that after the movie and its associated hits, the group's feet didn't touch the ground for four years. The recording of *Saturday Night Fever* became the biggest selling soundtrack album in history. So I wasn't alone in being impressed by the music. The Bee Gees enjoyed hit after hit on Robert Stigwood's RSO label – and were confirmed as kings of disco. John Travolta received an Oscar nomination for *Saturday Night Fever* but lost out to Richard Dreyfuss for *The Goodbye Girl.*

The power of the music and dancing of *Saturday Night Fever* stayed with me. Twenty years later *Saturday Night Fever* was again to re-enter my life.

In 1991, I started my own production company with a fellow actor called David Ian – and along with our co-producer Robert Stigwood – we had enjoyed a huge success with *Grease* at the Dominion Theatre in London's West End in the summer of 1993. The timing was perfect.

The West End had a number of shows running that were similar in style: *Les Misérables,* Miss Saigon and *Phantom of the Opera.* Audiences were looking for a family show, something they could take the kids to and *Grease* fitted the bill. All the kids knew the movie and loved the songs. All we had to do was produce a great show that did it justice and we succeeded.

So, with that in mind, we started talking about a follow-up. Robert had been thinking about doing *Saturday Night Fever* as a stage show for a long time and I let him know that I was very interested.

The movie was not a musical. It was a dramatic film with a strong, musical soundtrack. Although Travolta danced in the movie, he didn't sing the songs. None of the characters did. Robert Stigwood had the rights and I knew if he was involved that would mean a first-class production. He has never stinted on production values. A year earlier he had hired the American writer Nan Knighton to work on the script with Arlene Phillips, a great choreographer. Robert had originally wanted to do *Fever* as a Las Vegas spectacular with a band not unlike Take That supplying the music. Finally, Robert ruled out Las Vegas and, seeing the success of *Grease,* decided that

Saturday Night Fever should be staged in London as a legitimate West End musical. At the start of 1997 our company became an official producing partner with Robert. That was when the hard work really started.

I felt excited when I drove into Central London from my house in Highgate for a meeting at the Grosvenor House Hotel with Robert Stigwood, Arlene Phillips and David Ian. We had all been part of a successful production team with *Grease* and we were now hoping to repeat that success with *Saturday Night Fever*. Arlene and Nan Knighton had produced many draft scripts, the latest of which I was handed on my arrival for the meeting. I had never seen it until then.

I raced through the pages. There seemed to be one big problem with it. The basic concept. Robert and Arlene had hung on to the original Las Vegas idea. I just couldn't see that it would work with a group playing and singing the songs while the actors acted out the scenes. I had looked at the movie again prior to the meeting. When Travolta is walking down the street in the opening shot of *Saturday Night Fever* to the song 'Stayin' Alive' it's perfectly feasible that he could sing the song, rather than the Bee Gees. So why couldn't the *actors* sing?

When I suggested this there was a little bit of a 'Eureka!' moment. Arlene said, 'Of course'. Robert agreed and things started to motor from then on. The money was committed. We couldn't change our minds. I never believed that *Fever* had the instant family appeal of *Grease*. It had fantastic songs and had been a huge hit as a movie but it had some bad language and was quite raunchy in places. There were no guarantees of success. And we didn't have a star.

Here was I, a comparative newcomer to the production business, following my nose. There were to be times when I thought it was going to be bitten off. It was a testing experience for all of us and one that was to prove to me yet again that 'show' and 'business' are not always equal partners.

However, it did make me part of a 'starmaking' team – a new experience for me. My role as a fledgeling theatrical entrepreneur about to co-produce a giant £4 million London West End musical was one thing. The other was that £1 million pounds of my own money was going along for the ride . . .

1
Love and War

I've been a lousy parent but I was never an ungenerous one.

– Oscar Beuselinck Sen, 1995

My father Oscar was working for MI6 when I was born. He was in the Netherlands and I was four days old before he knew I had arrived. My mother Marjorie had left London during the worst bombing and was living with relatives in Peterborough. I was born there on 3 December 1945 and was three months old when we returned to North London.

Oscar was a difficult man to live with but he was always a determined and clever man, which made him useful to British Intelligence. He was self-educated, smart and good at languages. He never talked much about the war but he was there for the Allied landings. His attitude was that he had a good war: he had lived through it.

He was born in London in 1919, the eldest of four children. His father, also called Oscar, was a Belgian chef. My grandfather spent most of his life at sea, sailing between South Africa and England as head chef for the Union Castle Line. My mother was born in 1918 in the same street as my father in Endsleigh Gardens, Euston. Her father was a docker and when she was three, the family went to live on the Isle of Sheppey.

Oscar had always wanted to be a lawyer and when he was

fourteen he got a job as a tea boy with a firm of solicitors called Wright and Webb, in Bloomsbury Square. His thinking was there was only one way to go – up! He was working there when the war started and living with my grandmother Winifred, who had now moved from Holborn to Burnt Oak in North London. It was one of the first council estates built in the 1930s, and one of the largest in London.

Oscar met my mother – he called her Peggy – at the Mary Ward Youth Club in Holborn. After they married they went to live with his family, which included his sisters Yvonne and Lucy and brother Alfonse, at my grandmother's. That was the first home I knew. When Oscar returned from the war he didn't have any money but he was quickly back at work. He never went to university; he was self-taught.

It was cramped with all of us sharing a council house. There were three bedrooms and seven people living there, plus my grandfather when he came home from sea. The estate was open and rather nice, green compared to the middle of London. I felt happy there.

Things started to change when Oscar decided to buy his first house. It was a little semi-detached just off the Edgware Road in Colindale. It was a soulless, dreary place. Oscar couldn't afford the whole house, so we had to share it with someone else. There was an old woman called Mrs Mears living there with her daughter. There were three bedrooms, two living rooms and a kitchen. We shared the kitchen and had one bedroom and the use of one of the living rooms. I was always cold in that house. I used to sleep on a camp bed beside my parents. There was no central heating and everyone worried about me because I used to wet the bed a lot. My mum made things worse by putting a rubber sheet on the camp bed. This made it even colder.

Sadly, old Mrs Mears passed away. Unfortunately for us, she died in the bedroom next to ours. That night before leaving, her son, who had been there at the end, wished us a good night and pleasant dreams. We shivered all night. We were terrified! We slept with the lights on. Oscar was not the bravest man in the world.

Mrs Mears's daughter decided to sell up, so Oscar bought her out. We might have had more space but it wasn't enough for Oscar's personality. He was working to become a lawyer and doing it the hard way. Working as an articled clerk by day and studying at night. There was a small park nearby where he used to take his books and study. My mother was working for the Board of Trade as a typist. There were all sorts of pressures.

My grandmother, Winifred, lived about two miles away. When I was five years old, I would walk to her house every morning and have a cup of tea before going to school. She was a very strong woman and had long jet-black hair and piercing eyes. Whenever she wanted to chastise me she would open her eyes wide and stare. I used to crap myself because she looked like a witch. Despite this, she was always very kind to me and I loved her very much.

Oscar was thirty when he qualified and he went to work for the showbusiness impresario Jack Hylton. It was the start of what was to become a very successful legal career in entertainment. He loved it much more than he loved being at home.

My parents didn't have a good relationship. There was a lot of arguing. When it got too much I would run to my grandma's, go to the little bedroom in her house and pretend to fall asleep. I didn't want to go home.

I used to run to my grandmother's so often, she'd lock me out. She didn't want to interfere. I used to climb through the window. I even tried to pick the locks so that I could get in through the back door. It was not a happy time and I couldn't see it ever ending.

It got worse. They always seemed to be arguing over money.

My father was very easy with money and didn't care about it. My mother did. Both had come from quite poor families.

I was seven and they were arguing yet again about money. There were a few pounds sitting on the mantelpiece, so I took it, put it in my pocket and went upstairs to bed. I thought, 'In a minute they'll notice that the money isn't there and stop fighting.' They didn't. Eventually, I fell asleep and forgot all about it.

The next day I went to school and somebody asked me for a piece of paper. I put my hand in my pocket and pulled out a pound note. Then I pulled out another and another. The teacher saw the money and thought I had stolen it. I soon found myself standing in front of the headmistress, accused of stealing, and no one believed me. Luckily, my mum came to the school and supported my story. I was very relieved.

Oscar was trying to build a career for himself. He was young and had lots of energy. He didn't drink or smoke and he had no hobbies. What he did like was conflict. He was a bit of a trouble-maker. He would never cut the grass. Our garden was like a jungle. Our neighbours used to organize coach trips and Oscar took great delight in telling them that what they were doing wasn't legal. He loved to bait. Sometimes we would end up driving miles out of our way because a fellow motorist had done something he didn't like and we would end up chasing them. Talk about road rage! He would scream verbal abuse at the poor, unsuspecting motorist and whenever we got stopped by a policeman, he would remove his glasses and say, 'I think you should know that *I am a solicitor.*'

What saved both my parents was their sense of humour. They both had the ability to laugh at themselves. It is one of the few qualities they passed on to me, for which I am grateful.

The 1950s were drab. It seemed like one long, wet afternoon with ration books. Radio was the entertainment: *Life with the Lyons*, *Take It from Here*, *The Goon Show*, which I never really understood, and *Dick Barton – Special Agent*. Sundays were spent listening to *Two-Way Family Favourites* and *The Billy Cotton Band Show*. It was the time of Alma Cogan, Dennis Lotis and *Workers' Playtime*. Songs like 'How Much is that Doggy in the Window?' were storming up the hit parade. It was sixpence for the Saturday morning pictures. I loved the 'Flash Gordon' serials. And there was Hop-Along Cassidy and Laurel and Hardy – who were very slow and never made me laugh. Reading was the *Beano*, the *Dandy* and Dan Dare's heroic struggle against the evil Mekon in the *The Eagle*.

Occasionally, we went on family holidays to Belgium or to a boarding house at the seaside. But the real fun was when my mum used to take me to the local pictures. I loved the Hollywood movies, especially films like *Singin' in the Rain* and all those MGM musicals. They had terrific colour and great warmth. I loved the performers, the music, the dancing. I used to go home and try and imitate them by tap dancing on a tray or on the lino in my mum's kitchen.

The first live show I ever saw was *Kismet*. Another big hit at this time was *Paint Your Wagon*. The main song from the show was called 'I Talk to the Trees'. In it there is a line that goes 'I hang suspended'. I remember hearing that song the day that Ruth Ellis was hanged for the murder of her lover and I remember thinking, how inappropriate.

In 1953 I went to the Queen's Coronation with my mum and we stood there in the pouring rain, waving our flags. My most vivid memory was of the Queen of Tonga – an island in the Pacific Ocean – going by in an open-topped carriage waving to the crowds. She was the hit of the Coronation. She was a large woman, dressed in what seemed to me very little. She had a wonderful smile and a big personality. I had never seen anyone like her before. Sitting next to her in the carriage was a rather small man. Later, when asked who the small man was, Noël Coward reportedly quipped, 'Her lunch.'

Oscar was very musical. He played the piano and the violin and he used to sing filthy words to Gilbert and Sullivan songs. There was a piano in my grandmother's house and at Christmas he would play the piano and we would sing. Christmas was a nice time for the family. I always felt comfortable then because I knew when my parents were at my nan's they wouldn't row.

Oscar took me to see the *Crazy Gang* at the Victoria Palace. The show was presented by Jack Hylton. Hylton had once been a very successful band leader. Oscar told me of how one day on his way to a job, Hylton had turned to him and said, 'Forget this – I'll get some bugger working for me for a change.' And so his entertainment empire began.

Oscar was by now a young solicitor, making a name for himself and moving in literary circles. He was also an incorrigible charmer and women seemed to find him irresistible. In John Osborne's 1991 autobiography, *Almost a Gentleman*, he wrote of his first meeting with Oscar: 'I asked Oscar Lewenstein – a theatre producer – if he could recommend a solicitor. He knew someone he thought was just the man for me. "You'll like him," he said. "He's rather like you, in fact he's rather like Jimmy Porter [Osborne's character from *Look Back in Anger*]. His office is in Ludgate Hill and his name is Oscar Beuselinck.' Osborne goes on to list Oscar's sexual conquests of the day. Oscar appeared quite flattered when this was published, although he reluctantly conceded that Osborne had somewhat spiced up his exploits to make them appear more entertaining. Nevertheless, Osborne and Oscar were close friends for many years and both enjoyed a fondness for the irreverent. The last paragraph of Osborne's piece reads, 'You can't help liking him [Oscar], like Max Miller, no inner life to hinder.'

As far as Osborne's reference to 'inner life' is concerned, Oscar had a lot. He just didn't want anyone to see it. He was an enigma. He taught me to tell the truth and I have valued that all my life. I have always found it very difficult to lie. He once told me, 'At the end of the day, families are boring.' And he made no pretence of being a family man. My mother was unhappy most of the time but she was always there for me. Finally, they decided to call it a day. They separated.

I was thrilled. Delighted. No more fighting. No more shouting. The only thing that hinted at my theatricality was when they had these huge fights. I would cry and get very upset. I would then run upstairs and look at myself in the mirror crying. I was interested to see how I looked. I was my own audience.

Oscar sold the house and my mother and I went to live at my nan's. Then, Oscar had an idea. He brought home Jenny, the lady who was to become his second wife. She was an attractive twenty year old. Oscar's plan was that we would all live together! He seemed to want to set up the first hippie commune in North London with me and my mum. That idea got scotched very quickly. He seemed rather surprised.

Instead I went to live with my mother in a small two-bedroomed flat in St John's Wood. Oscar sent me off to a progressive, private school in Swiss Cottage. It attracted rich kids, rather than North London boys like me.

Growing up wasn't always easy. I would have liked to have had a brother or sister but that wasn't going to happen. The good thing about being an only child is that you learn to amuse yourself. That has stayed with me and I have never had a problem being on my own. If nothing else, I grew up a free spirit.

After Oscar left, my mother was bereft. It was as if she had been set adrift at sea. She was lost. She was going through an incredibly depressive time, totally fossilized within her own existence. Her husband had left her. She was trapped.

Although the relationship didn't work, it was still a relationship. You remove that and there's no crutch, you're isolated. My mother looked after me very well. I was always clean and smartly dressed. There was no deprivation but there wasn't a lot of joy in our lives. She couldn't motivate herself. She didn't know what to do. They had driven each other mad for fifteen years but without him she was stuck.

Meanwhile, at the fee-paying school run by an awful French woman, I was seeing a different kind of world, people with money, flashy cars and huge houses. It was all alien to me. I felt intimidated. It was a very cosmopolitan school. Suddenly I found myself mixing with American and Chinese children who seemed very sophisticated, something that I was not used to. I would get embarrassed that we didn't have a telephone. I used to give out a neighbour's phone number and if anybody called I'd say it was the butler who answered. It seems silly now but it was important to me then.

I had one good friend at the school, a boy called Peter Hoenig. His parents were German Jews who had managed to escape Hitler's Germany prior to the Second World War. His father was a psychiatrist. At weekends, I used to go and stay with Peter at his house in Kilburn. I think his father thought of me as a bit of a lost soul, for they invited me over all the time. We would have midnight feasts with the boys who lived next door – the Cockerell family. The eldest brother was Michael, who later went on to become a very successful television journalist. They seemed to me a very Bohemian family. They belonged to a group called the Progressive League and Peter and I joined them on the very first CND march from Aldermaston. They had a skiffle group and even some recording equipment. Most importantly for me, they had a microphone.

I started to get interested in music. I couldn't play any instruments so I began to sing a bit and record my voice on a big tape-recorder in their house. I was only twelve, but I had found something I really enjoyed. I had new friends, music and singing.

But then my father had another plan. Oscar decided to try for a reconciliation with my mother. They hadn't divorced, although Jenny was still in the background. Nevertheless, I was to leave my private school and we were all going to live as a family again in a new house in Edgware.

The reconciliation didn't last long. The marriage was finally put to rest by my mother. Oscar was up to his old tricks again and my mother had had enough. One day she picked up a vase and smashed it on Oscar's head. That was the end. The absolute conclusion of the marriage.

I was to continue my education at the local secondary modern school. I had been wearing short trousers at the private school and on the first day at my new school I wore them. Everybody thought I looked ridiculous. You didn't wear short trousers – aged 13 – at a state school. Everybody took the mickey out of me. They thought I looked stupid. I certainly felt it.

But I was with working-class kids and I liked playing football, so I got into the football team. I wasn't terribly interested in the academic stuff. What did interest me was that there were lots of girls, nice-looking girls.

I met a boy called Stuart Taylor. We bonded while playing with a dead fly and became mates. Stuart played lead guitar in a band called the Premiers and I went along to see them. I was very impressed.

I was spending time at my nan's and by now my mother had met a man called Lenny. He was a very nice man, who unfortunately had a weakness for drink. He just couldn't stop drinking. Lenny did not live with us all the time but he did stay over occasionally. I didn't like that.

The only bright spot was that Stuart and I had formed a

little group at school. I was the singer in the band and we were booked for a school dance. I was very self-conscious because I knew that the other kids thought of me as a bit of a nerd. I was the new boy who had turned up in short trousers. I was not considered an academic genius. I was quite good at sport and I was in the football team but that wasn't considered a big deal. Now, without fanfare, I was the star of the show.

It was the first time I ever sang in public. I sang 'Good Luck Charm', an Elvis Presley song. We were a big success. Suddenly, I became very popular with the boys but, more importantly, with the girls. I thought, 'This is quite good. I like this.' I had found something I could do. I liked the attention, being in the spotlight. I have never been interested in fame for its own sake but for what it can do for you. It can open doors, help make things happen. This was an early, small lesson for me.

I had been aware of rock 'n' roll since I was eleven. My nan had taken me to see Bill Haley in *Rock around the Clock*. What amazed me was seeing everybody jiving in the aisles of the cinema. I was not old enough to be a part of that but I was still very taken with it. Those were the days of Teddy Boys, drapes, sideburns and crêpe-sole shoes.

Music was now becoming more and more a part of my life. I was listening to modern jazz and musicians such as Gerry Mulligan and Chet Baker. At the same time I was buying records by Jerry Lee Lewis and Gene Vincent. I was glued to the radio. It was all very American. The hit show playing at that time was *West Side Story*. The first record I ever bought was Guy Mitchell's 'Singing the Blues'. It was a number one hit for many weeks.

My mother loved Frank Sinatra. My aunt was into German tenors and my father had a passion for Beethoven and Mozart. I was brought up a real musical mongrel. It was a wonderful education in music. I had all of the advantages and none of the prejudices.

Then, out of nowhere, the Premiers' lead singer left the band and Stuart asked me to replace him. I was 14 years old and we decided to change the name of the group. Out went the Premiers and we became Paul Dean and the Dreamers. Paul Dean wasn't interested in academic qualifications. He was a rock star.

2
Sutch is Life

He walks through the streets of London, late at night. The Ripper, Jack The Ripper . . .

— Screaming Lord Sutch, 'Jack the Ripper'

I was still at school but I was travelling to gigs all over the country and it was fabulous! We were playing 'covers' of songs by Chuck Berry, Cliff and Elvis and having a great time.

At school, the careers master had suggested I become a greengrocer. We were expected to get a 'proper' job. This was to be avoided at all costs. If we kept up the studying, we could keep the group going and avoid getting a 'proper' job. My grandfather had been a chef. Maybe I could become a chef. The only problem was, I wasn't interested in food. I had grown up on eggs and bacon but I roped in Stuart Taylor and we worked out a plan. The only thing open to us that we had any chance of getting was a catering course at the local technical college in Hendon. Strangely enough, I passed and so did he. I had never passed anything in my entire life before, so I was quite chuffed with myself for having achieved something in a semi-academic way.

I was still living with my mum in Edgware and travelling around the country with the Dreamers. We had a manager, a nice guy called David Oddie who ended up managing Status Quo. We went out for around £15 a night and if it was a really good booking and some distance away we might get £30. We had enough to buy a van out of the profits. We were a covers band playing the current hits of the time.

So things had worked out. It was high notes at night and rather flat soufflés during the day. At the college, we were obliged to dress as chefs – white jackets, check trousers, aprons and these ridiculous chef's hats. On the first day of term I walked into a room full of fifteen- and sixteen-year-old kids all proudly wearing huge chef's hats. They asked me where mine was and I made a feeble excuse. I had felt such a prat wearing it. I pretended that I had forgotten it. It was all bouquet garnis and bullshit to me. I lasted a term.

After technical college, I went to work for Oscar, arranging contract exchanges on houses and serving writs. I hated it. I once served a writ on a singer who was performing at the Orchid Ballroom in Purley. He was one of the Larry Parnes stable of singers, along with people like Billy Fury, Duffy Power and Johnny Gentle. Parnes was famous for giving his singers surnames that reflected their personality. The singer I was about to present the writ to for non-payment of bills was called Vince Eager. A very big guy and none too 'eager' to receive it. 'I've paid that fucker!' he protested. I didn't wait around. I slapped the writ in his hand and got out of there.

Oscar talked to me about going into the profession but I was not interested in the law. I got another job working in a solicitors' office in Golders Green but that lasted only three weeks. I did the same amount of time in a rawlplug factory in Mill Hill. It was next to a glue factory. I used to come out of there smelling to high heaven – but compared to the glue factory personnel I smelt like roses.

In the late 1950s the work ethic was very much nine to five and having a 'steady' job. Being in a group wasn't something to be taken seriously as a profession. All I wanted to do was play in the band. At least on stage I was able to express myself. Off stage I was shy. So being in a group was a perfect way of meeting girls. I was not good at chatting up girls. I could not walk across a dance floor and ask someone to dance. The fear of rejection was far too great. We were on display every night and, as the singer in a band, the girls would come to me and I welcomed them with open arms. It was our way of learning about sex and girls. Although I wasn't the one the girls found most attractive, one or two thought I was OK.

My sex life began at 15. She was a very nice girl of my own age, although she did look twenty-seven. I do not think, I must say, it was her first time and she had a reputation for being a bit of a goer. Luckily for me the rumours turned out to be true. She was a friendly girl and more than willing to give a young lad a good start. I was grateful for the tuition and this girl liked to practise a lot! Sex was not readily available when I was a teenager so I felt lucky to have someone introduce me to it. I am a patient man. I had been trying for two years.

After my first sexual encounter, things got better. Particularly with the girls who hung around after each gig. We did not call them 'groupies' but that's what they were. Sadly, there were not always enough to go around and, as the band travelled in one van, if you didn't pull you had to sit around and wait for that particular band member to return. Not only would you get irritated by having to wait around but you'd be even more pissed off by the fact that he'd pulled and you hadn't. So it became a competition between all the lads to see who could get a bunk-up. Very rarely did we all score at the same time. There was always one poor bastard who had to sit there and wait.

It was usually George the driver. Although not ugly, he had no teeth on one side of his mouth. To disguise this disfigurement, he spent most of the time talking out of the good side of his mouth, so it appeared he had a good set of teeth. We could never understand a word he said.

On the road there was never enough time to form a proper relationship with a girl. There was barely time to get her name. But there was plenty of sex and that's all we really wanted.

At 16 I decided to move in with my nan. Lenny was still living with my mother and Oscar was married to Jenny and living in Hadley Wood in Hertfordshire.

All I was interested in was the music. We decided to go 'professional'. This was an euphemism for not having a job. I was now singing full time. One such night we did get a lot of work but occasionally we had a night off. One such night we decided to go to a dance in Harrow to see another band. Little did I know that the guy performing that night would change my life. We went to see Screaming Lord Sutch and the Savages.

We'd been doing Cliff Richard numbers, safe, boring, reliable pop. And now I was watching the Screaming Lord. I had never seen anything like it in my life. I had never seen a man with hair down to his shoulders, let alone on stage doing rock 'n' roll. He was wearing a lavatory seat round his neck and large buffalo horns on his head and waving a long pole with a tuft of black hair dangling on the end at the audience. I was later to find out this was affectionately referred to as 'the minge pole'. The Savages consisted of a lead guitar, bass guitar, piano and drums. The sound they made was very loud, very raunchy rock 'n' roll. They were dressed as 'savages' in leopardskins. The Savages had always had great players like Richie Blackmore, who went on to play with Deep Purple and Rainbow, and Nicky Hopkins, who was a terrific piano player who ended up playing for the Stones. On drums was Carlo Little, an old friend of Sutch's and, at that time, the best drummer I had ever seen. The Savages were mean, moody and to me very charismatic. I was knocked out!

What I was so taken with was the theatricality of Sutch's act. The Screaming Lord came on to the stage with all his hair pinned up under his hat and halfway through the opening number he'd flip the hat off and shake his long, black hair into the faces of the crowd gathered around the front of the stage. The girls would scream with terror. They had never seen a wild man with hair down to his shoulders before. Certainly not a long-haired, raving lunatic who started real fires on stage as part of of 'Great Balls of Fire' routine. In 1961, in the patois of the day, it was 'blinding'.

We were used to people dancing to our music. They certainly didn't group round the front of the stage to watch us. It was all new and exciting to see the crowd standing at the front of the stage watching an act. It was a revelation, this was a pulsating, hard rock 'n' roll act with great horror moments, comedy with the buffalo horns and real flames as part of the act. It was completely insane. I had never seen anything like it in my life and I thought, 'God, this is fantastic! I want to be part of that.'

The theatrical aspects of the Screaming Lord captivated me. It was pure entertainment, all show; there was thought and preparation and hard work in the performance. It might have looked and sounded crazy but to get the logistics of such an act to the point where the audience are totally mesmerized by it involves as much planning as madness and magic. The only other band making its mark around London at that time was Cliff Bennett and the Rebel Rousers. Cliff used to do a fantastic impersonation of Jerry Lee Lewis but Screaming Lord Sutch was a self-created monster man.

With much of the musical life in the early 1960s, what happened or did not happen to your career was dictated by chance as much as by talent. And that's what happened with me. We were all fed up with Paul Dean and the Dreamers and we gradually drifted apart. Whilst messing about with other bands Stuart Taylor suddenly got an invitation to join Lord Sutch and he took it. I was still singing but I was bored and a little bit jealous so, I taught myself to play the piano, half hoping that Stuart might put in a word for me with Sutch. By happenstance, Freddy 'Fingers' Lee, who was the piano-player for Sutch, was leaving. It was a hard act to follow. 'Fingers', who had lost an eye in an accident with a dart, was quite a character. Stuart told me he was leaving and encouraged me to audition. I went to meet the Screaming Lord at what seemed to me to be a mansion in Harrow: a big, mock-Tudor house that he shared with his mum. We talked and then I played the piano. Sutch was happy. Stuart had put a good word in.

I was the new Freddy 'Fingers' Lee. And I was in the money. We worked six or seven nights a week and I was paid a fiver a night, which was good money. Sometimes we used to double our money by collecting the pennies that people threw at the stage. It was a dangerous business working for the Screaming Lord. And being Freddy 'Fingers' Lee. All Sutch's piano players were called that.

One night we were doing a gig in Oxford and I got a message that some bloke wanted to see me. This big, strapping guy appeared and said, 'Are you Freddy "Fingers" Lee?' I proudly announced that, yes, indeed I was. I thought that fame had finally come to me. He said, 'Yeah, well I'm so-and-so and you've got my sister pregnant.' I said, 'Pardon? What's her name?' He said her name and I said, 'No, no, no.' He said, 'When you were here before.' I said, 'No, I was never here before. You've got me muddled up. The Freddy "Fingers" Lee that you want is the previous Freddie "Fingers". He was livid. He thought I was messing him around. 'What do you mean, the previous guy?'

I replied, 'He only had one eye. As you can plainly see I have two. Why don't you go back to your sister and ask her if that Freddy "Fingers" Lee had one eye or two eyes?' He must have got the answer he wanted because I never saw him again. I had little time to dwell on it for Sutch kept us on move.

I would sing before Sutch made his entrance, introduce him and then be his stooge. My life seemed complete.

At home things had settled down a bit. Oscar and my mother had divorced and she was getting alimony. She was also doing some secretarial work for the BBC. So, financially, if not emotionally, she was healthy. I was earning good money and paying 'rent' to my grandma. And most nights of the week, I was a 'Savage' being brutalized by Screaming Lord Sutch. What a wonderful life!

I have never been a follower of fashion but when you are a teenage boy you want to conform. I was into button-down shirts and winkle picker shoes. It was a rowdy time for music. This was the first British pop revolution. This was prior to the Beatles.

I might not have been a natural slave to fashion, but I had to be for Sutch's act. As well as wearing leopardskins, the band wore orange shirts, black cords, white cowboy boots with bells on and bleached hair. So I had to bleach my hair white.

As Paul Dean, I had worn traditional suits or red jackets with a little bow-tie, very straight and boring. With Sutch everything in excess was success. But we were part of a big attraction. People were paying good money to see us. We felt like stars. I loved it and I loved the fact that it was crazy. It was far from boring. Sutch was a wonderful madman.

He used to do a number called 'Jack the Ripper' in which he'd come through the crowd like Count Dracula. His face was painted white and he wore a big black cloak, a boxed period hat, carried a medical bag and sang his 'Jack the Ripper' number. I would dress up as his victim. I wore dodgy old wigs and silly dresses. Stuffed inside my dress was a large red heart and and a set of rubber lungs. About halfway through the number, Sutch would grab hold of me, throw me on a table, produce a very large, dangerous-looking knife and plunge it into my chest. Then, slowly accompanied by a ripping sound effect on the guitar, he would slice me open, thrust his hand inside and produce the pair of rubber lungs which he would wave in the faces of the audience. The girls and the boys – although they didn't like to admit it – were terrified. They loved it and, happily, so did I. Without realizing it, I was beginning to learn about comedy and performing.

It could also be terrifying because the local herberts came to the shows looking for trouble. So, although being a member of Sutch's band was exhilarating, it was also frightening. On one occasion we had hold of Sutch by his feet while the local bad boys were holding him by his cloak. Sutch was in the middle being strangled. They were trying to pull him off the stage and we were trying to keep him on it.

There were bouncers in some of the places we played but not always. We used to see lots of fights and when they started we simply kept playing. There was nothing else you could do. The violence could be anywhere. An out-of-the-way place in Gloucestershire could be as 'rough' as any London club. It was wild and it could get dangerous. I once saw a girl stick a glass in another girl's face.

Musically, this was a limbo period, leaving behind Teddy Boys, skiffle, Tommy Steele and the 1950s. There was a new feeling around in the early 1960s.

Nevertheless, Sutch was his own fashion. He never had a hit record but most people knew about him because he was so good at organizing publicity stunts. My first recording experience was with him in a studio in North London. It was with the legendary Joe Meek.

Joe Meek was a tall, gentle man from the West Country who had managed to create a unique sound and I was somewhat in awe of him and the whole recording process. Sutch was not the greatest singer in the world and Joe was very patient and kind up until the point when he felt the Screaming Lord was never going to sing in tune. Then he would become very agitated and let Sutch have it in no uncertain manner. He had been a BBC sound engineer but had earned money from writing the 'B' side of a Tommy Steele hit record. He started Triumph, his own record company. His first hit was 'Angela Jones' by Michael Cox and he had a Number 1 with John Leyton singing 'Johnny Remember Me'.

Cliff Richard and the Shadows were massive. The Shadows had enjoyed a string of instrumental hits and Meek wanted some of that action. So he created the Tornadoes. They had backed Billy Fury but then put out their own records. It was at the end of 1962 that 'Telstar' was an enormous success. It was Number 1 in Britain and the Tornadoes were the first British group to get to that spot in America before the Beatles. Meek was also recording a group called The Outlaws who later became Chas and Dave. Joe Meek was a powerful man by the time I turned up with Sutch and company at his studios – two rooms above a leather shop – in the Holloway Road where we recorded 'Dracula's Daughter'.

For Sutch, 'Dracula's Daughter' was, like his other recordings, not a chart success. It was 'Telstar' not 'Dracula's Daughter' that is recalled as Meek's greatest recording. People remember that song more than Sputnik 1, the first satellite, which the 'Telstar' song was about. Sadly, on 3 February 1967, Joe Meek shot and killed himself after murdering the woman who ran the leather shop below his studio. No clear motive was ever established. Such was Joe's impact on the music scene that there is still an appreciation group for him called the Joe Meek Society.

David Sutch was never intimidated by the lack of Top Twenty success. He lived and breathed publicity. At one gig the locals got so caught up in Sutch's act that they went beserk and completely wrecked the hall. We managed to escape offstage and out the back door. Instead of getting out of the area, Sutch ran to the nearest phone box to call Fleet Street and gave the national newspapers the story of our close brush with death. We were about to be killed but Sutch wanted his name in the papers. I noticed a gang of lads were coming down the road, angry and heading straight for us. I shouted, 'Dave, let's get out of here!' He just turned and said, 'You coward.' Then he ran for it. He was 23 and I was six years younger. After that I always checked the escape routes offstage. Just in case.

Nothing bothered Sutch and certainly not people in power. He stood against Harold Wilson in a by-election in Huyton, near Liverpool. This was the beginning of the Monster Raving Loony Party. I always admired their defence policy: 'No one should sit on de-fence.' His campaign involved me running around the constituency in a leopardskin shouting, 'Vote, Vote, Vote for the Screaming Lord!' That Christmas we all received a card with a picture of the Screaming Lord shaking hands with a slightly bemused Harold Wilson.

He was making a lot of money. In those days he used to earn between £150 and £200 a night. Not bad for the early 1960s. We were the Savages with Screaming Lord Sutch and I would have done it for nothing.

But I felt I had been doing it a long time. When you are a teenager every step of your life seems like *for ever*. I had been singing in this pop business for three years – a long time when you are only 17. I was living with my grandma and running around the country with Screaming Lord Sutch. I was also doing that other teenage thing – staying in bed all day. My grandmother had a very piercing voice and used to shout, 'Come on, Paul', to get me out of bed. We had a budgie called Nelson and when I finally got up the bird would continue to drive me mad with, 'Come on, Paul. Come on, Paul.'

I escaped to Germany with Sutch along with lots of British groups. We got a booking at the Star Club on the Reeperbahn in Hamburg which was open around the clock. That is where

I first encountered the Beatles. They were the big stars of the club. Sutch was booked in as a kind of rock/horror act. I found the whole scene as strange as the audiences found us. There were the prostitutes advertising their wares in windows of the Reeperbahn and you could buy guns openly in shops. I was wary of it all. But they loved the British and the Beatles were the kings of the place. Sutch's act went down OK but the crowds were more interested in drinking when we were on and did not really get the act.

That is when I decided I had had enough of Screaming Lord Sutch. It was the usual thing that happened in bands. The Savages started to suffer from delusions of grandeur. We thought that we were just as important as the Screaming Lord. That we would leave Sutch, nick the name and present ourselves as The Savages. Of course – quite rightly – the Screaming Lord wasn't having any of it. The Savages was the name of his group and would remain so. So we left and called ourselves the Soul Savages. We were booked as a rock 'n' roll attraction. We still wore the leopardskins and did a bit of an act. It was enough to get us on package tours as support artists for groups like the Who and Herman's Hermits.

Beatlemania had begun. Everywhere people were wearing Beatles outfits and Beatles haircuts. We were ever so slightly out of our time dressed in leopardskins! But we were different enough to get work with acts such as Del Shannon when he came over from America. We would do our thing before Del came on and performed his hits like 'Runaway'. I would do the comedy as the Soul Savages in the first half and later when the star came on we would back him.

As Paul Dean and the Dreamers we had this guy who used to follow us to gigs. He had the sweetest face, with big brown eyes. That sweet little innocent turned out to be none other than Keith Moon who was by now beating the hell out of the drums with the Who. They were the first 'mod' band. Pete

Townshend was using feedback on his guitar, Keith Moon was the wild man of drums, Roger Daltrey had a great rock voice and sang original songs. And amid all this mayhem was bass-player John Entwistle who stood stock still, expressionless and was affectionately known as 'The Ox'. At the end of their act they would smash their instruments and wreck the stage. I never understood how the group managed to replace their instruments every night. They must have had great deals with the manufacturers. But they were terrific and a nice bunch of guys. These were the high spots for me and, without realizing it, I was always being drawn to the dramatic. To the groups with real acts.

It was a good time. I was relaxed. We were winning. We were not a star attraction but we were working. Relaxation was going to watch Georgie Fame and the Blue Flames down at the Flamingo or listening to John Mayall and Eric Clapton play down the Scene. I was singing and learning all the time. It was great but it was not enough for me. We were doing big shows but I felt like a poor relative on the tours. We were the same age as the stars. The big difference wasn't age. We didn't have a hit record. We were sitting around one night after a show and Peter Noone, aka Herman of the Hermits, announced, 'Why don't we all sing our hits.' We didn't have any hits. I was deeply pissed off by that. I thought, 'This is shit.'

The nearest thing we'd come to stardom was backing Screaming Lord Sutch. I didn't really believe that much in myself as a singer. I have a good baritone voice which is suited to theatrical shows but I didn't have a high rock voice – the kind you need to be a pop singer. When we did cover versions of songs, I could never do them in the original key. Doubts were creeping in everywhere. We decided to lose the leopard skins and change our image to a more modern look. So we changed our name. We became the Thoughts. Not terribly exciting but we were obviously doing a lot of thinking.

I was 19 and I felt I was getting old. We still hadn't made it. We did a tour of Denmark but we were more into the girls than the music. We went to Germany but didn't rehearse properly and the promoter sent us home. We had been doing it for what seemed a lifetime. We were a successful touring group but we had no hit record and no record deal.

Our big mistake was that we didn't write our own songs. Groups in the South of England didn't get into songwriting like they did in the North. The Beatles and the Hollies wrote their own material.

We were winding down as a band and were about to call it a day. One of the last gigs we played was the Market Hall in St Albans. Stuart Taylor had a new girlfriend called Angela who was a hairdresser. Angela bought along a friend who was also a hairdresser called Susan Gee. She was 16, had big blue eyes and a lovely smile and, by my standards, seemed rather posh. Little did I know that she would become my wife and the mother of our two children.

3
Radical Times

Let the sunshine in.

– the *Hair* finale

My grandfather had retired from the ships and my nan took every opportunity to give him a regular ear-bashing. He had been away for fifty years and she was making up for it. Her voice boomed and very sensibly he got a job at the local hospital as a cook to escape. I was a singer, living with my nan and grandfather in a council house on an estate in North London. A very noisy council house.

It was at this point that my father returned to further complicate my life. He and Jenny had married and, as usual, Oscar had a masterplan. He was doing very well. He was a lawyer for MGM Films and represented Sean Connery, Richard Harris and the Beatles. He was also involved with Woodfall Films who had just made *Tom Jones* with Albert Finney. It was directed by Tony Richardson who was then married to Vanessa Redgrave, with a screenplay written by Oscar's friend John Osborne.

Oscar was financially sound enough to buy a large house in Letchmore Heath, a beautiful village in Hertfordshire. It had a big garden, a stable block and a cottage in the grounds. My father invited my grandparents and myself to move into the cottage and we did. My motive was clear: it was cheap and I got my meals cooked. But I was living with my father, his new wife, my grandparents and Ted – Oscar's driver – his wife and clutch of children. Ted had lived next door to my nan for years and the benevolent Oscar had hired him as his chauffeur. A recipe for disaster as Ted and my nan had never got on. It was no wonder – now that Oscar was back in it – that I was beginning to consider what my life was all about. And Robert Stigwood was about to make his first impression on me.

Robert was 30 and had arrived from Australia in 1957. He had worked in advertising and then organized a P. J. Proby tour which had failed. Robert had been declared bankrupt. He was beginning again and had his own record label. He was looking for singers and acts to manage. I was introduced to Robert in a pub in Soho by a mutual friend who managed bands. We got talking and he decided he wanted to promote me. I told him that my middle name was Oscar. So that's who I became: 'Oscar'.

Robert was also involved with the Who. Actor Terence Stamp's brother Chris was managing them. Chris was friendly with Michael Douglas who was working as an assistant on the film *The Heroes of Telemark* with his father Kirk and Richard Harris. Chris Stamp asked Michael Douglas if he wanted to put any money into the Who, who were still a fledgeling act. To his everlasting regret, he did not take up the offer.

But Robert was forging ahead and I was part of his big plans. Robert got Pete Townshend to write me (as 'Oscar') a song called 'Join My Gang'. It was a nice song. Robert had decided he was going to make me a star. He was also getting involved with Eric Clapton and was beginning to build his empire. He had a deal with Polydor to put Oscar's records out. I made this album of romantic songs. I thought I was Frank Sinatra and it was ridiculous and a waste of money. It was philanthropic of Robert to indulge me, but we still had hopes for a hit with 'Join My Gang' as a single.

I wanted a hit. I was willing to do anything to promote it. It was suggested I take the *Queen Elizabeth* to Cherbourg and get married on board to some girl who was to be part of the publicity stunt. I was all for it. The Beatles were making it big and I thought, 'Yeah, Yeah, Yeah!' Thankfully, that idea didn't take off. And neither did the record.

I was given every chance. We had promotional pictures taken, a PR man and a plugger called Brian Lane – who went on to become a major rock manager – were hired to promote the record. Robert even went to the trouble of having plaster cast busts of my head made, calling them 'Oscars' and presenting them to radio stations and the media as a promotional gimmick. The record made it into the lower regions of the Radio London charts but it was never a genuine hit.

I heard myself on the radio for the first time, which was very exciting. So we tried again and I made more records with Robert. The best of these was written by David Bowie. There had been a string of prison breaks and gaol security had become a national joke. Robert had Bowie write this song called 'Over the Wall We Go'. It was a very funny song: 'Over the wall we go/All coppers are 'nanas.' It suited me because instead of trying to be a rock singer, this was more of a comedy song. David Bowie did a bit in the middle and it worked really well. It also got me on television with appearances on variety shows like *The Ken Dodd Show*.

Robert was now working with Brian Epstein as managing director of Epstein's NEMS Enterprises, which controlled his enormous stable of stars led by the Beatles, Cilla Black, Gerry and the Pacemakers and Billy J. Kramer. Success was all around me. However, I was no longer flavour of the month. I had a proper contract and three records, 'Club of Lights', 'Join My Gang' and 'Over the Wall We Go', none of which were major successes.

Robert had worked very hard to try and make me a success,

but by now he had bigger fish to fry. Eric Clapton and the Who were soaring and a new group that Robert had brought over from Australia called the Bee Gees was demanding all of his attention.

They found something for me. I went to Belgium for the Knokke Festival Song Contest. It involved a team of artists from different countries performing against each other. I was on the British team with Roger Whittaker and Gerry Marsden, along with two female singers, Lois Lane and Dodi West. I was still Oscar. We won and Roger Whittaker won the overall best artist of the show.

Brian Epstein had come over to watch. He took us all out for dinner and it seemed to me that he was drinking a lot and, for a man at the height of his success, he didn't seem overly happy. In contrast Robert Stigwood was flourishing and involved with the Bee Gees and the Cream as well as running his own record label. I was sidelined and had nowhere to go.

Luckily, I had met Susan. She lived in Radlett, not too far from Letchmore Heath. Her parents lived in a very nice detached house at the end of a crescent. Her mother was rather cut glass – not unlike Daphne, the mother in *Just Good Friends*. Suddenly, out of nowhere, there I was, a right scruff, driving round to pick up their daughter in an old Rover that farted. They really didn't like me and they showed it. I wasn't even allowed to walk up the garden parth to knock for Susan whenever I wanted to take her out. I used to wait in the car and sound my horn. They couldn't wait for her to finish with me, but their longing to see the back of me had the reverse effect. It made us even more determined to see each other.

Oscar's attempt at being the family patriarch had led to a volatile environment and I was very unhappy and depressed. My grandmother had an extremely loud voice; my father had an even louder one and the combination was unbearable. My mother was now living in Russell Square in London and I continued to live in Letchmore Heath.

The combination of Oscar and my nan coupled with the fact that the group was more or less redundant, meaning that I was spending more time at home, was beginning to drive me mad. I was starting to suffer from giddy spells and found it difficult to breathe. I decided to do something about my emotional state. I was very lucky as my local doctor – a woman called Dr Randall – was very sympathetic. She let me pour my heart out to her. I just wanted to talk to someone and she took the time to listen.

I had spent years running here, there and everywhere without ever really achieving anything and I think I had reached the end of my tether. I was very confused. Not focussed. It was the usual problems of growing up. I didn't know who I was, where I was going or what I was doing. On top of that, I wasn't eating properly. Dr Randall checked me out and found nothing physically wrong with me. It was stress and I realized that the only person who could help me was myself. A valuable lesson that I have never forgotten.

And I had Susan. She was wonderful. Someone I could hold and cuddle. Someone I could love. I had never had a regular girlfriend and she was a normal person, with a normal family, who lived in a normal house. At home, the environment was perpetual tension. The only constant thing in my life was Susan.

Everything changed when she found out she was pregnant. My life had been unorthodox but Susan lived in the world of net curtains and what-would-the-neighbours-think? These were different times. You either had the baby adopted or you got married. We did not discuss abortion. I was 20, Susan was 17. We decided we were going to tell her parents that she was pregnant and that we were going to get married. Susan's eldest sister was also planning to be married in three months' time and Susan was to be a bridesmaid. Now Susan was to marry first. We talked and talked and worried about confronting her parents. What would they say? How would they handle it? We arranged to meet them.

We went in nervously and, in their neat front room, I summoned up all my courage and made the announcement. 'I'm afraid to say that Susan is pregnant . . .' Silence. 'We would like to get married.' Because of Susan's age we needed their permission. Her mother looked at her father and said, 'Oh, Ted. What about the bridesmaids' dresses?' I thought her response was a little odd. She seemed more concerned about Susan fitting into the bridesmaid's dress for her sister's wedding than the fact that she was pregnant. I suppose they were in shock. They had worked very hard. They had both come from humble backgrounds. All they had ever wanted was the best for their daughter. They wanted a proper wedding, to a proper man, at the proper time. They did not want their daughter marrying a man who appeared to have no future.

I was confused but I felt that I was doing the right thing. I had a pregnant girlfriend and I was going to marry her. I had no job. I had no home. The only hope I had was Oscar. I had no chance of a bank loan or mortgage. No matter how much the bank wanted to listen, they wouldn't be listening to me in those circumstances. So I asked Oscar to lend me the money to buy a house. I made it clear it was a loan, not a gift.

Oscar was never interested in money. He liked to tip, to be magnanimous. He did not care about money per se but there was a touch of the Godfather about Oscar. He looked after things. He'd do you a favour and then remind you about it for the rest of your life. He was forever reminding me, 'I bought you an amplifier when you were fifteen.' However, I had no choice and accepted the loan gratefully.

I wanted a proper home for Susan and the baby and found

a four-bedroomed house. Somewhat ostentatious for a 20 year-old kid with nothing in the bank. It was in Redbourne near St Albans. Oscar paid £9,500 for it and we moved in. I could see the neighbours thinking, 'How could *they* afford *that?*'

Susan's mother was there to help Susan but she was never happy with the situation. They just couldn't understand me. A scruffy individual without a regular job, with a father who was successful and owned a big house, much grander than their own. It did not add up. It was terribly confusing for them but they had to accept the situation.

We got married at Watford Registry Office and I was late for the wedding because of the traffic. Oscar was pacing up and down outside when I arrived saying, 'In here! Get in here!' Susan wore a very nice white suit and I wore a dark blue, double-breasted reefer jacket. It was a small affair. Susan's parents, Oscar and Jenny and my grandparents.

After the ceremony we went for a jolly meal. I was more concerned about the future than the meal. I had to look after Susan and the baby. I had to get a job. I had to be responsible. I thought it through. I was going to get a job. I had no shame. I spoke to Oscar and the conversation went like this:

'Thanks for the money for the house but now could you help me get a job?'

'Yes, what do you want to do?'

'I don't know, something to do with music.'

'I know a music publisher.'

This was Robert Melon, an American who ran his own music publishing company, Melon Music. Oscar set me up with an interview at his office in Bond Street. Melon Music controlled songs like 'Stranger on the Shore' by Acker Bilk and had a really good back catalogue of hits. I was hired by Robert Melon to find new writers and songs and exploit his existing catalogue of music.

47

We were now living in Redbourne and I had a job. A budding music publisher, commuting to London every day. And then the baby arrived. It was the middle of the night when Susan's waters broke. I rushed her to St Albans Hospital and Natasha was born after seven hours' labour. Fathers were not allowed in the delivery room in those days, so I waited at Oscar's for news of the baby's arrival. She weighed 7 pounds 4 ounces and she was beautiful.

I was now a dad. I was making reasonable money, £25 a week. I had expenses as well so, financially, it was a good arrangement. However, I felt a bit like a door-to-door salesman hawking tired old songs to record producers. I needed some excitement. I decided to find a new group. A group to record, not to sing with. I tracked down a band called Wainwright's Gentleman. They came from Sudbury near Harrow. I listened to them and thought they had something. I played a tape of them to Robert Melon and he agreed I should pursue the project.

I signed them up to Melon Music and we renamed them the Sweet Shop and I got them a record deal with Decca. Now all we needed was a hit. The publicity man for Decca at that time was Les Perrin. He handled a string of names. We needed to attract some publicity to combine with the release of their new debut single which had been produced by Phil Wayman, who also worked for Robert Melon. Phil was later to achieve great success as the band's producer, as well as running his own recording studio. I had an idea.

I contacted a company in the North-West who made jelly babies. The Beatles had at one time expressed a love of jelly babies and as a result, this company had enjoyed great success. Unfortunately for them, the Beatles had now moved on from jelly babies and the company was looking at ways to improve their profile. I told this chap at the sweet manufacturers, 'I want you to make me the world's largest jelly baby.' He said, 'How big?' I said, 'Eight feet!' He said 'Jesus, we'll have to make a special mould.' And they did.

My idea was to go to a children's hospital with the world's largest jelly baby, plus packets of sweets for the kiddies and invite the press. That was Les Perrin's job. I began to worry that the giant jelly baby plus the group might not be enough to attract the world's press. So to cover myself I thought it would be a good idea if we could make the jelly baby in the image of a well-known celebrity. Simon Dee was a major television and radio celebrity and hosted *Top of the Pops*. I thought to myself, 'He's the man.' So I called his agent – Bunny Lewis – and told him of my plan and to my surprise (and because it was for a charity) he agreed to do it. I then called the man at the sweet manufacturers and said, 'You know that eight foot jelly baby your'e making me?' He replied, 'Yes.' I said, 'Could you make it look like Simon Dee?' There was a silence. He then said, 'Fuck me! I'll do my best.'

The big day arrived and we all trooped to Great Ormond Street Hospital – the group, Simon Dee and the eight-foot jelly baby which was pink and looked nothing like Simon Dee. Unfortunately, Les Perrin – the publicist – hadn't done the business and no one turned up. Save for one journalist from the *Confectioners' Gazette* who was incredibly excited with the scoop of a lifetime. None the less, the group and Simon Dee to their credit, along with the eight-foot jelly baby, visited the children – who were delighted to see them – and handed out packets of sweets. The Sweet Shop became the Sweet and went on to have great success throughout the world as a glam-rock band with hits like 'Ballroom Blitz'. I never found out what happened to the eight-foot jelly baby.

I was now 22. I was losing a lot of weight and I was unhappy doing what I was doing. I wasn't performing. Performing for me is a great release. A great way to exorcize the demons and I was not doing that. Instead I was taking my anxieties out on Susan.

Then early in 1968 I read in the *Daily Express* about an outrageous show that was playing on Broadway and about to come to London. The show was extremely controversial. There had never been anything like it. It had four-letter words and something even more shocking: nudity. The show was called *Hair*. Robert Stigwood was one of the producers. Robert had by then bought Associated London Scripts (ALS), which involved him in the management of Frankie Howerd, Rita Tushingham and Lionel Jeffries as well as Tony Hancock's writers Ray Galton and Alan Simpson, who created *Steptoe and Son*. He also had the talents of Johnny Speight which meant Alf Garnett too. Robert had a lot to do. There was a *Till Death Us Do Part* film and Frankie Howerd in *Up Pompeii*. Nevertheless, there was always time for new enterprises and *Hair* was one of them.

I had not been in contact with Robert Stigwood for more than a year but I called him and he kindly arranged for me to audition for *Hair*. It was an open call. At the audition there was this nervy, enthusiastic guy in glasses running around, organizing things. He was the assistant stage manager and it was his job to introduce the actors to the creative team. His name was Cameron Mackintosh. He later became a world-class producer with shows like *Cats*, *Les Misérables*, *Phantom of the Opera* and *Miss Saigon*.

I sang 'I Who Have Nothing', the old Shirley Bassey song because I thought it would show off my big voice. Luckily, I got a recall. I went through a series of auditions and finally they lined us up across the front of the stage. It was like a scene from *A Chorus Line*. A meat market. 'You go. You stay. You go. You stay.' They got to me: 'You *stay*.' It seemed to echo. Thank God. I was in. I have never ever seen casting handled in such a way, apart from the movies and the auditions for *Hair*.

Hair had originally opened off Broadway as part of Joseph Papp's New York Shakespeare Festival. Jerome Ragni and James Rado were a couple of out-of-work actors who got together with the composer Galt MacDermot and created a musical celebrating the hippie culture. Many young Americans were disenchanted with the conservative values of their parents and America's continued involvement in the Vietnam War. *Hair*'s main protagonist, Claude, cannot make up his mind as to whether to protest against the war – 'Hell no, we won't go . . .' – or to leave the hippie 'tribe' and fight for his country.

Director Tom O'Horgan, who founded the La Mama Company in New York, took the off-Broadway production, restyled it and made it work within the parameters of a Broadway show. On 29 April 1968 the 'American Tribal Love Rock Musical' opened at the Biltmore Theater in New York. *Hair* was on Broadway. It was fresh and very different. It was a new form of musical theatre. A rock musical with something to say. It seemed appropriate in 1968. The Year of Revolution.

In Britain, the Establishment was still running things. Robert Stigwood's gamble was that part of that Establishment – the Lord Chamberlain's office – would soon be abolished. With my father's help, he had bought the UK rights to *Hair* prior to the Lord Chamberlain's demise in September 1968. Until that moment, what concerned the producers was whether the Lord Chamberlain would allow the 'bad' language and the infamous nude scene.

For the writers the nudity was simply an honest expression of truth. For the producers it was an honest expression of box-office.

Nudity was one problem for the censor but there was also a lot of swearing in the show. There was a scene that tried to demonstrate that 'bad' words are basically sounds. I would say, 'I hate the fucking world.' Another character would add, 'I hate the fucking world.' I replied, 'Fuck, fuck, fuckity, fuck,

51

fuck, fuck.' The audience found it funny. It was there to illus-
trate that it was fucking silly to get upset about the word
'fuck'. The show was about truth and it was those ideals that
made the show a hit.

There was of course – and the producers were well aware of
it – the shock value. There was a commercial aspect to the
nudity and bad language that was used in the show. However,
there was no way that the Lord Chamberlain was going to let
that happen on the London stage. I was put on a retainer with
the rest of the cast for three months while we waited for the
Lord Chamberlain's office to be abolished. The producers
knew this was imminent.

I was terribly excited about performing again, especially in
the theatre, which was nearer to my heart than I had realized. I had always been drawn to acting and half fancied
myself as an actor but lacked the confidence to do anything
about it. Events had pushed me, given me the shove I needed.
When I began rehearsals in July 1968, I knew for the first
time in my life what I wanted to do. I had found a home.

It was luck and timing. *Hair* was a freewheeling show and
my lack of experience didn't matter. If somebody had been
putting on *Oklahoma* I would have found it difficult because
I lacked the stagecraft. For *Hair* they were looking for kids off
the street rather than for 'actors'. It was a complete salvation
for me to stumble into a show where the main requirement
was to be young, look the part, be reasonably attractive and
able to sing. I qualified on all counts. I was ahead of the game.
I was not a total off-the-street and I had a big enough voice
within the context of the show. The soft rock theatrical *Hair*
songs were perfect for me: I sang them in the keys in which
they were written. They were rock-based but weren't true
rock 'n' roll, although it was marketed as the first rock
musical.

Thirty years later I still don't know how much influence

Robert Stigwood had for me – but he enabled me to get through the front door and after that it was down to me. No decent producer uses anyone to be kind. There is no charity. The show, the total package, is always the most important factor.

It was a whole new world. And a new me. I didn't find out until some years later that Oscar had negotiated the rights to bring *Hair* to London for Robert Stigwood. When he did the deal he knew nothing of my interest in the show, but he did know about the content, the drug references, the language and the nudity. When I got involved he did not want the family name associated with that. It was a matter of business. He thought it might affect his work with his high-profile clients. He was concerned about his professional reputation which he had spent a lifetime building up. He was at the height of his fame as a lawyer representing MGM, the Beatles and rising stars such as John Thaw. It was heavy-duty stuff and I could see his point about being associated with a controversial show. I think his other consideration was that I wouldn't be very good in it.

In 1967 the first film I was in happened through Oscar and his connection with Woodfall Films. It was titled *Red and Blue*. It was directed by Tony Richardson and starred his wife Vanessa Redgrave. I had one line which was 'Quelque chose the Beatles?' That was it. So, as far as he was concerned, *Hair* was my first venture into high-profile, serious showbusiness. He said he didn't think Beuselinck was a good name to launch oneself into the British theatre with. He also told me, 'I've sued a lot of people and I don't want anyone saying to you, "You're the son of that bastard lawyer – I'm not giving you a job." ' I think he was afraid I might embarrass him with his clients. And I had met and liked some of them. I was especially impressed by John Thaw. He had been in the television series *Redcap* for four years but had just made *The Bofors*

Gun with Nicol Williamson when I met him. They were buddies and real, legitimate actors. John Thaw was a nice bloke. He and I talked a lot about acting and it was interesting for me. Everywhere I turned I was learning about the theatrical world. And also learning to play the game.

So 'Paul Oscar Beuselinck' became 'Paul Nicholas'. Which was how I was introduced to the interesting bunch of people on *Hair*. I was cast as Claude and the other leading character, Berger, was played by Oliver Tobias. Tim Curry – before *The Rocky Horror Show* – was one of the tribe, as were Elaine Paige and Murray Head, who was to be the original Judas in *Jesus Christ Superstar*. There was also a girl called Marsha Hunt. She was one of the most exotic people I had ever met. She had her hair in an enormous 'Afro'.

Hair was a show of its time: peace, love and the world of protest. By the time it had reached London in the late 1960s, it might have been a little after its time. However, it was a celebration of cultural and ethnic identity. It was a time when blacks were very heavily into their roots.

The Black and White Minstrel Show was playing at the Victoria Palace in London. One of the cast members of *Hair* was a 40-year-old black American woman called Gloria Stuart, who took great exception to *The Black and White Minstrel Show*, which depicted white males in black faces and curly black wigs representing negro minstrels. Their appearance was deeply offensive to many black people.

Gloria decided to audition for the show. When she arrived back later that day, she was fuming. The producers had told her she was not quite the right colour. Apparently, she wasn't dark enough. Undaunted, Gloria returned to the Victoria Palace, this time armed with a placard protesting against the show. I am sure that her efforts contributed to the demise, shortly thereafter, of *The Black and White Minstrel Show*.

As for me, I was the star of a West End musical, the type of which had never been seen before. I could hardly believe it. My life was changing. *Hair* was opening my eyes to all kinds of things.

There had been a rigorous rehearsal period which I had found very avant-garde. It involved getting 'in touch' with yourself. It was all very touchy-feely. Very un-British. We were exploring each other and ourselves. It was good for me. It helped me learn to open up. During the seven weeks' rehearsal, I felt truly happy. It put me where I wanted to be. Up until then I was sure of the destination; I just didn't know the route.

I might have graduated to musical theatre but it would have been difficult without training. *Hair* was the key. It unlocked a world of musical theatre that, without knowing it, I had been looking for. I was 23. Most of the cast were in their late teens. I was married with a child. Getting in touch with myself was very good for me but disastrous for my family.

Hair opened at the Shaftesbury Theatre in September 1968. People would enter the auditorium and be welcomed by the 'tribe' offering flowers and greetings of 'peace' and 'love'. A strong smell of incense hung in the air. It was a really different experience for theatregoers. They were being invited to participate in not just a show but a 'happening'.

The music began gradually with the house lights still on, with the mystical sound of guitars and bells wafting through the theatre. And slowly, very slowly, the tribe began to move down the aisles, over the seats of the audience, towards the stage, where I sat wrapped in a blanket like a Red Indian chief.

When the moon is in the seventh house,
And Jupiter aligns with Mars.
Then peace will guide the planets and
Love will steer the stars.
This is the dawning of the Age of Aquarius . . .

'Aquarius', 'Hair', 'I've Got Life and 'Let The Sunshine In' – they were recorded by many artists, who quickly became aware of the quality of the songs.

The first outrageous moment in the show was a song called 'Sodomy'. It was a send up of all the sexual prejudices and hypocrisy of Church and Establishment. It involved the cast adopting sexual poses in a religious context to demonstrate the lyric of the song.

> *Sodomy,*
> *Fellatio,*
> *Cunnilingus*
> *Paederasty,*
> *Father why do these words sound so nasty?*
> *Masturbation can be fun,*
> *Join the holy orgy*
> *Karma Sutra*
> *Everyone . . .*

Many of the audience got up and walked out. The rest of them didn't know what the hell we were singing about. I certainly didn't!

The first half finished with the famous nude scene. There was never an empty seat, for no one quite knew what to expect. The curiosity factor was a huge marketing device. It was a beautiful scene and very tastefully done. The song – aptly titled 'Where Do I Go?' – reflects Claude's dilemma. Should he leave the hippie commune or join the army? It was four minutes long. Towards the end of the song, the cast would disappear under a huge white, silk sheet that covered the stage and remove their clothing. At the climax of the song and the word 'freedom', the cast would reappear from beneath the sheet and present themselves to the audience naked. It was meant to convey that 'we are all one and naked in the eyes of

God'. The lighting was such that the actors felt comfortable doing it. However, as the years went by – and people got more used to nudity – the lighting got somewhat brighter. I was the guy in the middle of all this, singing the song. It's funny but no one ever remembers me. I wonder why? However, I was quite relieved. I wouldn't have been thrilled about taking my clothes off in public. I would have found it embarrassing, especially when I saw the competition from some of the other lads who were standing there.

The second act highlight involved a take-off of the Supremes, who were famous for wearing shiny, sequined blue dresses. Marsha and two other black girls sang a song called 'White Boys', extolling their virtues. It was a direct counterpoint to a number in the first half sung by three white girls called 'Black Boys' with the same message. Marsha and the girls were revealed on a moving platform that was trucked down to the front of the stage. It appeared to the audience as if they were wearing three tight-fitting blue sequined dresses *à la* Supremes. At a crucial moment in the song, the girls parted to reveal that they were in fact wearing one large blue sequined dress. The audience found it hilarious and it was a real show-stopper.

The end of the show was truly a wonderful finale. The audience was so swept up that when 'Let The Sunshine In' – this plea for world peace – climaxed the performance, the audience climbed on to the stage and joined the cast singing and dancing. It was not planned. They just did it spontaneously. It happened every night. It was a tremendous breakthrough for theatre. Even musical theatre was still perceived as rather formal.

Hair involved the audience and they had a fantastic time. Princess Anne came. She had a friend from school in the show called Rowan McCulloch, the daughter of Uncle Mac, who I had listened to as a child presenting *Children's Hour* on the radio. Princess Anne saw *Hair* three times and always danced on the stage. She loved it.

I received a fan letter from David Niven: 'What a wonderful show, keep up the good work.' We were visited by people like Katharine Hepburn, Gregory Peck, Sidney Poitier, Paul Newman, John and Yoko, many stars from the entertainiment world. My most treasured memory was of meeting Judy Garland who was nearing the end of her life. She was a slight woman, like a little sparrow. Tiny, fragile, but warm and friendly. She took the trouble to visit everybody in the cast. We were *the* hit show. Everyone was talking about *Hair*.

By now Susan and I had been married for three years. In 1969, Oscar was born. He was named after my grandfather who had recently died. When the baby was born, there was so much love and hope. His arrival helped our relationship – but not for long.

Obviously a bad hair day.
Me at 18 months.

Father and son: Oscar and
I at the beginning of our
loving if sometimes
difficult relationship.

An early school photograph.
Aged seven.

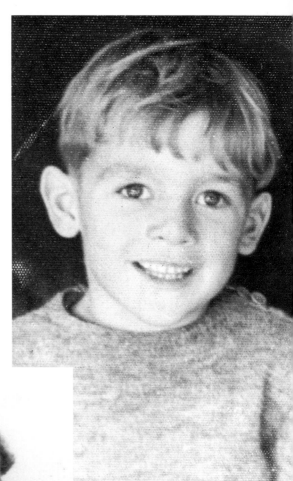

Nice pair of legs. Mum's aren't bad
either. Aged 11 on the beach in Belgium.

Paul Dean and the Dreamers (left to right, Paul, Ray, Pete, me and Stuart Taylor). *(Above)*

My days as a teenaged rock 'n' roller. *(Below)*

As one of Screaming Lord Sutch's Savages resplendent in leopardskin. *(Right)*

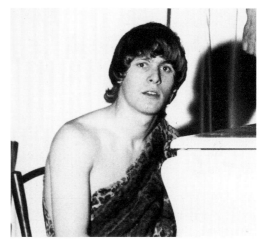

Playing the piano and singing with the Savages as the new Freddy 'Fingers' Lee. *(Below right)*

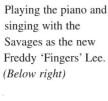

Screaming Lord Sutch letting his hair down and giving it some. *(Bottom right)*

It was not a big affair: the wedding supper. From left there is me, Susan's mum, my grandfather, Oscar's second wife Jenny, Oscar, Grandma Winifred, Susan's father and Susan. *(Above)*

Susan and I on our wedding day. *(Above)*

Susan and I with baby Oscar (our second child) the day after he was born in April 1969. *(Right)*

Playing the part of Claude in the first rock musical *Hair* at the Shaftesbury Theatre (1968).

Linzi and I in our first photograph. We met while touring with *Hair*. (*Top right*)

'Jesus Christ Superstar,
do you think you're what
they say you are?'
Stephen Tate's Judas
questions Christ's
motives. *(Right)*

'Everything's alright.'
Dana Gillespie as Mary
Magdalene comforts Jesus.
(Below)

The first time that we rehearsed the crucifixion, I cried. I was completely overcome. It just hit me: the brilliance of the music, the brilliance of the show.

This is how Andrew Lloyd Webber and Tim Rice looked when I first met them. Tim inscribed the photograph: 'To Paul, who was to become my favourite J.C. From your favourite lyricist,' (Andrew wrote, 'Where's the picture of you?')

Alf Garnett is awed by Dana Gillespie's cleavage when she and I appeared (as off-duty Jesus and Mary Magdalene) on *Till Death Us Do Part*. Alf was distracted when searching for signs of my stigmata.

4
Stuck Together

We haven't got any glue, Paulie.

– Paul Barber, 1971

F or the first time in my life I had found what I wanted. I thought this combination of acting and singing was something that I could do. I was 23 and I was being paid £100 a week. Good money. *Hair* also got me a movie.

I was given time off from the show to co-star with Jane Birkin and Serge Gainsbourg who were the Continental Sonny and Cher. She was the English rose *chanteuse* and he was all Gauloise and designer stubble. That, at least, was the image. They had a big success with the record 'Je t'aime moi non plus'.

We made a film called *Cannabis* which did indeed go up in a puff of smoke. It was an intriguing experience. It was a French production and also known as *Les Chemins de Katmandu* and I never discovered what it was all about because it was all in French. I played Serge's American side kick. We were drug dealers.

Before filming began I went to meet Serge and Jane, who had been married to the Bond composer John Barry. I went to their flat, which was completely black. All the rooms and floors were black. Everything was black. I thought, 'This is weird' – but that was before we went to dinner.

He could barely speak English and I couldn't speak French. They took me out to dinner to a very flash restaurant and all they served at this restaurant were flowers. I am a North London boy brought up on eggs and bacon. So I asked for a few chips. They were served with my rose petals and daffodils. It was horrible. But the chips were good. He was tremendously charming. Jane was my age, 24. They were a very nice couple.

The films scenes were not so easy. I tried to learn French phonetically but I got in a terrible mess. I was dubbed in French and Serge was dubbed in English. When we did scenes together, neither of us was ever quite sure when to speak. We laughed a lot. It was a terrible film. But they were huge stars in the late 1960s and I learned something about filming.

I was in France for seven weeks and I was still trying to make the marriage work, so Susan came out to visit me. I have a picture of the two of us asleep on the film set but it was one of only a few peaceful moments in our relationship at that time.

Marsha was different. She was black, American, very hip and interesting. It was a time when women were beginning to become more independent. Men could have women friends other than those they slept with. What was relevant was that she was very strong and sophisticated. We enjoyed each other's company. She was also connected; she attracted people. She had worked with Elton John and knew Mick Fleetwood. She was much more hip, more of a celebrity, than I was; she circulated and was on the cover of *Vogue*. I was a little kid from a council estate and you're either comfortable in that celebrity environment or you're not. I'm not and never have been. I get satisfaction from the work. I don't get it from the party afterwards. To me, this was further evidence of a relationship at home that wasn't working. Susan and I did not laugh enough together. We did not talk enough together. The only thing we had in common really was our children. *Hair* saved my life and destroyed my marriage.

Hair was the toast of the town and members of the cast were invited everywhere. The genie was already out of the bottle. The boundaries of taste were changing by the day. It was the time of those revealing photographs of Germaine Greer – this highly educated lady displaying her naughty bits. Nudity was seriously fashionable.

The vanquishing of the Lord Chamberlain and the success of *Hair* led to a series of similar shows. Robert Stigwood produced *The Dirtiest Show in Town*, which had nudity and was quite radical.

More famous was *Oh! Calcutta!* which Michael White co-produced with Kenneth Tynan – the doyen of theatre critics. Tynan convinced John Lennon, Samuel Beckett and Sam Shepard to contribute to the show. It involved lots of nudity and outrageous sketches. Arlene Phillips performed a 'nude ballet' in it. At the end of the performance the cast would stand on stage, completely naked and say, rather smugly I thought, 'This show makes *Hair* look like *Mary Poppins*.' It laboured the point that they were attempting to be radical and funny.

On its first night at the Royalty Theatre, I was sitting with Kathleen Tynan and Michael White when a man shouted from the stalls to all the naked bodies on stage, 'A pound for the first one who farts.' Everyone looked very embarrassed. I thought it was tremendous.

Kathleen Tynan – the wife of the first man to say 'fuck' on British television and one of the creators of this infamous nude revue – was rather appalled. The man had got the biggest laugh of the night. It might have been a liberal time but there were certain things you did not say or do and this was one of them. The fart joke was considered over the top!

This was a pivotal time in my life, a time of radical change and *Hair* was allowing me to do everything I wanted in the theatre at that point. I worked as the artistic director, which meant I went in and watched the show, rehearsed the cast and re-auditioned for people who left.

I gave Patti Boulaye her first job long before she won *New Faces* in 1978. She was 16 when she went on a visit to Madame Tussaud's and joined a queue, not realizing that the line was for the *Hair* auditions at the Shaftesbury Theatre. She came in and sang, of all things, 'The Sound of Music'. She was good; she was used to singing back home in Nigeria. But unlike Marsha she was not into Afros. She was more conservative with plaits and a silk dress. She could sing but she didn't want to take her clothes off. I gave her a job, she did not take her clothes off and she never ate the marijuana cake the cast baked for her on her 17th birthday. She was a very straight lady and I liked that.

I got involved in more auditions when the producers asked me to play Claude on tour doing long runs in places like Manchester and Liverpool. They wanted an experienced lead who would also help them pick a touring cast.

At one audition I saw one of the most beautiful girls that I have ever seen in my life. She was of mixed race and very slim. She was completely gorgeous and I instantly became attracted to her. I found out some facts about her. Her name was Linzi Jennings and she and her sister Jeanne had grown up in a part of South London called the Borough. Her mother Jessie was from Bethnal Green and her father Ken was from Guyana in Central South America. Before joining *Hair* she had been a secretary but, luckily for me, had decided on a career change.

I acquired all this information from one of the other girls in the show. I was too shy to talk to her myself. The girls that you really fancy are the ones you can never talk to. I could talk to all the other girls but around Linzi I would get very tongue-tied.

There was one small problem. She was not remotely interested in me. To her I was just another scruff in the show. My jeans were tied up with string. She had a point. I was everything she didn't need. The only glimmer of hope was that her friend liked me. So at least I had a reason for hanging round. Another problem: she had a boyfriend. I spent six weeks of rehearsal time trying to woo her but nothing would work. I was too shy to simply ask her out.

She had recently returned from a German production of *Hair*, where she had played the part of Chrissy as well as one of the trio of black girls who sang 'White Boys'. I was one white boy she was clearly not interested in.

We went on tour and in Manchester I was sharing digs with the actor Paul Barber, who was an 18-year-old kid then. Everyone knows him as a regular on *Only Fools and Horses* and as one of the stars from the *The Full Monty*. I had found out that Linzi was staying with two other girls from the show, in the Lincoln Service Flats in Manchester, and I managed to wangle a flat above Linzi's and shared it with Paul.

After the show, the girls from the flat below – Linzi included – would come to our flat where we would then sing to a guitar or watch television together. I would try and be at my most charming on these occasions. I was trying to be clever and funny and did not notice that I never stopped talking, especially during the dramatic bits on television. I was an irritating so-and-so and she later told me that I used to drive her mad. She was very proper and vanished on the dot to her own flat downstairs every night.

I knew I was beginning to fall in love with Linzi, but she seemed so unobtainable. There was nothing showbusiness or pretentious about her. She was very down to earth and honest. I had fancied her since the moment I first saw her and I was with her night after night during the show. So close, yet so far. Ten weeks went by. The only thing in my favour was that she had realized that I was not a dirty hippie. That I was clean. In fact I bathed every day. Cleanliness was to be my triumph. Much more than my witty repartee during TV time!

One night as usual the girls had been watching television in our flat and around eleven o'clock Linzi had decided to go to her flat so that she could hear the end of a programme that we had been watching. I had been talking all through the programme trying to get attention. Later, at about two in the morning I was in the room with Paul and we were fooling around and broke a lamp. We needed to fix it, stick it together but Paul said, 'We've not got any glue, Paulie.' Quick as a flash I said, 'Maybe they've got some glue downstairs. I'll just pop down and see.'

I knocked on the door. Luckily she came to the door in her nightdress. It was now or never!

'Have you got any glue?' I asked.

'I'll go and have a look,' she said.

Does it get more torrid than that? I doubt it. At the start it wasn't something from either a Jackie Collins or a Jane Austen novel. Linzi made me a cup of tea. We talked, I started to get romantic and we didn't get out of bed for three weeks. The glue obviously worked!

I had a lot of pent-up emotion. I fell desperately in love with Linzi. I knew that she was the woman for me, this was true love. We resolved to be together. It was 1970 and I had found the person I wanted to be with.

Divorce proceedings began. Susan did not want to stay in Redbourne but I had some money in the bank and we sold the house for £18,000 making a profit of £7,500. I paid Oscar the £9,500 he'd lent me. The profit went towards setting Susan and the children up in a new house in Elstree. Linzi and I rented a one-roomed flat in Muswell Hill in North London for £10 a week.

The tour of *Hair* had ended and I then became the artistic director of the show in London. Linzi was in the cast. It was a bit of a stretch with money. The children were going to fee-paying schools now. I was living with a girl that I was very much in love with. It was not perfect but the kids were happy. Susan was a terrific mother and I saw a lot of the children, every week without fail. We never lost contact but I still felt bad about leaving them. One of the reasons why I didn't have children early on with Linzi – apart from the financial considerations – was that I felt it would be disloyal to Natasha and Oscar.

There is a wonderful song written by Barry Manilow called 'Sunday Father and Son' about fathers taking their kids out for the day, picking them up and taking them to the zoo and then having to drop them off. It wasn't easy.

Susan had been left with two young children. I had gone off with another girl. Susan felt hurt and had every reason to do so. I saw them all the time and it was very important to me that I did. I felt guilty leaving but I knew the alternatives were far worse. Two people living together for too many years, making each other unhappy and consequently making their children unhappy. We were both too young. What was important to me was that I didn't lose contact with my children. The kids used to come and stay with me, and Linzi was there from day one. She and I used to take the kids out together, so they got to know her really well. She was never pushy with the kids, or tried to take their mother's place, or create any rivalry. None of that nonsense. I was happy. I was able to support them and keep Susan in some comfort. There are no winners in divorce. All you can do is try to make it less painful.

Linzi had to adjust to a man with two children, someone else's children and be supportive to their father. Susan never interfered with my contact with the children. This young girl whose life had been completely turned upside-down would always invite me in for a cup of tea. We shared two lovely children.

5
Superstar

The backbone of any musical is the story.

– Andrew Lloyd Webber, 1984

'**G**od! That's fantastic.'

The words were out of my mouth before I quite knew what I was saying. I was enjoying *Hair* and Murray Head, who had remained with the show, had just played me his recording of *Jesus Christ Superstar*. The Bible is packed with good stories but this song reflected the most potent one, the last seven days of Christ's life.

Murray had recorded the album with Ian Gillan of Deep Purple. It had been written by two guys I had never heard of: Andrew Lloyd Webber and Tim Rice. There was a cracking song, brilliantly sung by Murray as Judas, but it also had an intriguing title, 'Jesus Christ Superstar'. Years on we glibly trot that out as a very easy title, but in 1971 to call Jesus Christ a superstar was daring.

Lloyd Webber and Tim Rice started working together as teenagers in 1965. They had used the Bible as the source for *Joseph and the Amazing Technicolor Dreamcoat* which was a pop cantata originally written as a school concert piece. It was good enough to get them involved with David Land who until then had received most of his income from the Dagenham Girl Pipers. Land had a partner, property developer Sefton Myers, and together they were New Talent Ventures.

Andrew Lloyd Webber and Tim Rice were certainly talented

71

and new, but no one could have imagined to what height their work and fame would reach. What Murray Head had played for me was part of their take on Jesus of Nazareth. The idea was of a celebrity story – Jesus as a star who is put on a pedestal and finally discarded by his fans.

It was novel and clearly controversial. It was also timely. The rock opera *Tommy* by the Who, a 90-minute recording, was selling incredibly well. Tim Rice said their influence was *Hair* rather than *Tommy* but it was the record sales that gave them an edge when it came to pushing *Jesus Christ Superstar*.

The money was made available, £14,000, to make a demonstration record, and hearing Murray's track from that was my magical introduction to Andrew Lloyd Webber, Tim Rice and *Jesus Christ Superstar*. Murray has a great voice and had worked with Joe Cocker on his celebrated cover version of the Beatles' 'With a Little Help from My Friends'. Tim Rice had known him from his days at EMI Records and that connection proved so positive for me.

MCA Records did a double album of *Superstar* in October 1970, when David Land was looking for a company to produce it as a theatrical extravaganza. His friend Leslie Grade had warned him about the subject matter, suggesting it would offend Christian and Jewish communities. Harold Fielding, who was famous for shows like *The Music Man*, was regarded as the theatre's musical mastermind and Land took the project to him. He was enthusiastic and a deal was almost done – the contracts were called up but not signed.

When Murray Head played me his version of 'Superstar', I thought, 'Sounds like a hit to me.' I took the song to Robert Stigwood and played it for him. Robert has a fantastic nose, an instant nose, and when he goes, like all terrific entrepreneurs, he goes. Robert sought out Andrew Lloyd Webber and Tim Rice and his enthusiasm was such that they were convinced he was the one to produce *Superstar*. They talked David Land into going with Robert and the package abruptly changed tack. It would be a very different production to the formal opera envisaged by Harold Fielding.

The album, which featured Mike D'Abo as Herod and Paul Raven (before he became Gary Glitter) as the priest, was very successful in America and Murray's 'Jesus Christ Superstar' got into the Top Fifty. The album sold more than 2 million copies in less than a year. There was a demand for a live stage version. In fact, there were unofficial versions being staged before Robert intervened with plans for a Broadway production.

Tom O'Horgan, who had directed *Hair* and continued to shock audiences with *Lenny*, his theatre interpretation of the life of American comic and drug addict Lenny Bruce, would direct. Robin Wagner was the set designer. The show opened with Jeff Fenholt as Jesus and Ben Vereen as Judas Iscariot. It was huge – primarily because of the concept of Jesus as a superstar. It was also a brand new world of musical theatre. No one realized just how innovative this was.

From editorial pages and pulpits there were strong reactions on the merits or demerits of *Superstar*. It was, of course, all good for business at the Mark Hellinger Theater in New York. Religious groups picketed West 51st Street but no one really knew who was under fire, being attacked. Was it blasphemous? Was it anti-Semitic? I did think and still do believe it was simply a brilliant piece of musical theatre when staged correctly. Some critics thought that Tom O'Horgan's production in New York was too elaborate, too fussy. Clive Barnes, who had the title 'Butcher of Broadway', had a go and so did the *New York Times*, which wrote that the set was 'like the Christmas decorations on a chic Fifth Avenue shop'. Andrew Lloyd Webber and Tim Rice were not happy with what they saw as the over-the-top nature of the Broadway show.

They were set on something much simpler for London and brought in Australian Jim Sharman as director. He had guided *Hair* and *Superstar* in Sydney where he was also renowned for a production of Mozart's opera *Don Giovanni*. His reputation was enormous, but he was the opposite: pleasantly low key, a shy man. In 1972 they began to cast *Superstar* for a London production. I wanted to be the first Jesus in Britain – well, the second.

The difficulty was that I am a natural baritone. The role of Jesus was a great challenge. The music was far more demanding to sing than *Hair*. It had a classical feel and was very new and different. Ian Gillan – who had done the album – is a rock singer who sings in a high tenor voice. Andrew Lloyd Webber, like most composers, wants his music to have presence. He writes high vocals. Most rock songs, other than maybe a few by artists such as Neil Diamond, are set in a high key. Most really great rock singers have high voices and Ian Gillan's on the *Jesus Christ Superstar* album was no exception.

I had a problem. My solution was to use a lot of falsetto, particularly for the high notes. I thought I had managed to make it sound effective. I certainly hoped I had when I went to the auditions at the Palace Theatre. The original meetings had been at the Shaftesbury Theatre where *Hair* had played for three years, but the roof had fallen in and *Hair* was taken off. Maybe it was the ghost of the Lord Chamberlain. However, *Hair* had survived 1,997 performances. I was involved with lots of the *Hair* cast in raising money to save the Shaftesbury. It was our thank you to a theatre that had been good to us.

Now, I wanted a miracle at the Palace. First, I met this nervy, rather jumpy chap who turned out to be Andrew Lloyd Webber. He was a dandy, dressed to the nines in velvet and a cravat. With him was this tall, witty and more easy-going man who was Tim Rice. The funny thing about those two was that they are so English. So *very* English. They were with David Land – their typically Jewish manager – who when things didn't going well, was often heard to exclaim, 'Who pissed on the chips?' They comprised a remarkable team.

It was the beginning of something massive for all involved and I sensed that during the seven auditions. What I didn't know at the time was that they didn't want me to play Jesus, although Andrew had patiently helped me with some of the songs. Robert Stigwood told me that later. He also said he had fought for me. In fact, for more than twenty-five years he has been telling me he fought for me to get the role. He knew I could sing it and it was a time of enormous change in the musical theatre. Before *Superstar*, performers were pigeon-holed as either actors, singers or dancers. They were not thought capable of flexibility. Because of the Lloyd Webber and Cameron Mackintosh shows we accept 'sung-through' productions where you have to be able to act and sing as in an opera. In 1972 this was a brand new concept. No one had ever done a commercial West End show like it.

There was a lot of speculation about who was going to play the title role. More than three thousand hopefuls had auditioned for Jim Sharman, Tim and Andrew and it was used to help market the show, 'Who will play Jesus?'

I had been the lead in *Hair*, the first rock musical show, a production that had to wait for the Lord Chamberlain to be abolished before it could open. Now I was up for the lead in another ground-breaking show. I still hadn't got it.

The hardest part is always getting the job. I was and am adaptable. The problem for me has always been that big singing parts are not normally technically within my range. It is not that I can't sing them but I do not sing them in the keys in which they should be sung. I got away with it only once and that was with *Superstar*.

I was acutely aware of the singing problem when I went along to audition but I also knew that I was coming off the back of a big success, which does not hurt. People like to associate themselves with success. I had the Jesus beard and long hair. I looked physically right, gentle but steely. I had spent an awful amount of time sitting in that little room in Muswell Hill practising with Linzi's help. This show was something that I really wanted to get. The standard of singing in the early 1970s was such that there was only Gary Bond – who did *Joseph* at the Young Vic – and a few others, myself included, who could play it. But, as luck would have it, by June 1972 I *was* Jesus Christ Superstar.

I was 26 and I was also naïve. I had this very sensitive role and when I turned up for a press call at the Palace Theatre I parked in a no-parking zone: 'Jesus Breaks Law' headlines never occurred to me.

They presented me to the press as if I was a lottery winner. The photographers and reporters elbowed each other out of the way. They fired questions at me so fast I felt I was in one of those *Deadline Midnight* Hollywood movies. I was freaked by it. The photographers shouted, 'Jesus, look this way!' 'What are your religious beliefs?' asked the reporters. I had not been prepared or advised about what might be asked, or coached in appropriately clever answers. I was in the spotlight. I was also on the spot. I managed to blurt out that I was not very religious, did not go to church, had been brought up in the Church of England and had gone to Sunday school. I didn't say it was to play snooker and table tennis. I wasn't quite that naïve.

I hadn't been prepared for the overwhelming interest in me. It was my first brush with fame. With *Hair* we had no billing outside the theatre as performers. The costume designer had billing out front and when they sacked her, her billing remained. Which always amused me. I wasn't aware of the importance of billing then. Or handling the press.

After all the questions in the bar of the Palace Theatre the photographers asked me to go outside for more pictures in natural light. I went with them and was almost knocked down by a van! One of the theatre people went white. It was that close a call. He needed a drink so we went into a pub. The photographers followed and we did a deal. Yes, they could take my photograph drinking a pint of beer, if they left after it. The next day the newspaper showed pictures of 'Jesus' drinking a pint of beer in the Coach and Horses. It had been my first public day as Jesus Christ Superstar. There had been such a fuss that I had not been able to gather my thoughts. I believed it was not so much a religious show as entertainment.

The first major difference from the Broadway production of *Superstar* was the set. In America it had been very intricate and biblical. Jesus appeared out of a huge artichoke effect and his followers appeared climbing over a rotating wall. Spectacular! In London the set was like the 'Last Supper' by Salvador Dali. Blocks of light would rise up and take on various shapes. It was simple and so different from the world of *The Greatest Story Ever Told*. It was a contemporary set. The designer, Brian Thompson, later designed *The Rocky Horror Show*.

Jesus Christ Superstar had something that I don't believe Lloyd Webber has ever recaptured. There was a rawness to the music, a youthful daringness about it. Andrew's work has mellowed with age. With *Superstar* it was dangerous. It was a dangerous piece of work. A dangerous title.

When we started rehearsing I was not sure how to play 'Him'. Should I play him as a spiritual leader? A healer? It was Jesus seen through Judas's eyes. Judas asked:

Tell me what you think about your friends at the top,
Now who d'you think besides yourself's the pick of the
crop?

77

Buddha, was he where it's at – is he where you are?
Could Muhammad move a mountain or was that just
  PR?

For me there was a sense of Jesus's self-glorification in the
way it was written. It was radical. The music was sensational.
It was the first time a rock opera had ever been performed on
the West End stage. Like *Hair* it was an event. It was a mile-
stone and a beginning of something that was going to perme-
ate throughout the West End for three decades to come. This
was the coming of *Jesus Christ Superstar*, Tim Rice, Andrew
Lloyd Webber and the British musical. Until that moment we
had always played second fiddle to America – other than the
occasional outing like *My Fair Lady*. Broadway came to us; we
rarely went there.

It was the birth of so much and I was there. It was my
second job. I had no formal training as an actor or as a singer.
I don't think I would get the job if it was being cast in 1999,
but this was the beginning. We were all learning how to do it.
Tim Rice once told me I was the best 'Jesus Christ' he had
ever seen. I said, 'I bet you say that to all the Jesuses.' And
there have been many.

There's always a warmth for the original cast. Paul Jabara,
an American, who had also been in *Hair* was cast as Herod.
He was outrageous. Paul had problems getting a work permit
and chained himself to the railings of Number 10 Downing
Street with a placard that read, 'I must have this job.' It
worked. He made himself such a nuisance they gave him a
permit. Paul – like Victor Spinetti, who also played Herod –
arrived on stage in a giant, inflatable bed, surrounded by
beautiful women. It was a wonderful scene and gave the show
the moment of comedy it needed.

Stephen Tate was Judas and he played him as a student
rebel. Only a couple of weeks before we were due to open in

previews Sylvie McNeill, who was to be Mary Magdalene –
she won the role over more than five hundred other
contenders – walked out. We never knew why, other than she
said it was a family matter. Dana Gillespie was brought in.
She received an enormous amount of attention and it wasn't
just because of her voice. She did have a big voice and an even
bigger bosom. She was an extraordinary woman. She had
been the British Water Ski Champion for four years up to
1967. She spoke with a very upper-class accent. I think she
was a baroness. She could certainly sing 'I Don't Know How to
Love Him' as Mary Magdalene.

Andrew Lloyd Webber and Tim Rice are perfectionists.
Although they had written *Joseph*, it had not been produced
in the West End. This was their first West End show and they
were, quite rightly, very nervous.

We were all in the spotlight. On the first night we had a
host of protesters singing hymns and waving placards with
'Jesus Is Not a Superstar' and 'Jesus Christ Super Sham'. It
did not help first-night butterflies.

Although I was not religious, the defining moment for me
was dealing with the first time that I was crucified on stage.
I was already tense, nervous about the scale of the production.
Playing Jesus in a brand new musical.

I saw the 1997 West End production at the Lyceum
Theatre. In it the actor playing Jesus drags the cross around
on his back for quite some time. The cross is then laid on the
stage and Jesus is put on it. Then they lift it. The audience
knows what's coming. There is no sense of theatre about what
is going to happen.

What was wonderful about Jim Sharman's production was
that I was taken away to be crucified. I went below the stage.
I sat on a bicycle seat which was attached to a thin cross-
shaped frame. I adopted the crucifixion pose and in doing so
masked the frame. Then slowly I rose up through the centre

of the stage. There was smoke and wailing music. And as I was revealed to the audience, it looked to them as if I was hanging in mid-air. The audience saw this apparition floating up and it blew their minds. Jesus says:

God forgive them –
They don't know what they're doing
Who is my mother?
Where is my mother?
My God! My God!
Why have you forgotten me?
I'm thirsty I'm thirsty!
Oh God I'm thirsty!
It is finished.

Jesus is stabbed with a spear. Simultaneously the choir and orchestra crescendo and, as Jesus is dying, the sound dies with him to a last breath. Jesus prays, 'Father into you hands, I commend my spirit.'

Jesus dies and the theme of 'Gethsemane' plays. It is a beautiful theme, played at a slow tempo on cellos and violins. It is incredibly moving. The audience was transfixed and the only sound other than the orchestra that could be heard was that of the audience weeping.

The first time we rehearsed the crucifixion, I cried. I was completely overcome. It just hit me, the brilliance of the music, the brilliance of the show.

Technically, I have always believed that, other than 'Gethsemane', Judas had better songs. Jesus had the Crucifixion. A moment in theatre. It was beautifully staged and encapsulated everything that was good about that partic-ular production. It was simple and that's what made it work. The American production was fussy and extravagant. It didn't allow the music to breathe. The cornerstone of the show was the music and lyrics. And of course the story.

You cannot win playing Jesus. Everybody, whether they are religious or not, has an of image of what their Jesus looks like. And most probably it's not you. When I came out of the stage door, I was dressed in jeans and there were always people waiting for me. I had fans in *Hair* but this was different. I felt they wanted more than just an autograph. That some were taking it too seriously, too much to heart.

As soon as I lit a cigarette and headed for the pub, any expectations of my religious qualities were quickly dispelled. The worst thing for me playing Jesus was to curb my natural sense of wanting to be a little bit naughty. The only time I gave in was when a chap in the front row sneezed. I couldn't resist: 'God bless you, my son.'

I said it in such a way that only about the first six rows heard it. The big problem was there are not too many laughs in the show and it is difficult, when you are doing eight shows a week, not to break it up. There are actors who will always play around, corpse a little bit. I don't mind a laugh on stage but not as Jesus. I felt I absolutely had to be the part otherwise I would have destroyed it for the audience.

It was the making of Andrew Lloyd Webber and Tim Rice and it was the beginning for me. The show had mixed reviews. Benedict Nightingale gave me a terrible notice in *The Times*. I was so angry, I was going to write to him and I said to Oscar, 'This guy has given me an awful, unfair review. I want to write to him'. Oscar dismissed this nonsense with, 'Don't be ridiculous – that's part of the game. You have to be able to take it.' And I did.

Many people make fun of Andrew Lloyd Webber and they say, 'Oh, Andrew nicks things.' It's nonsense. Andrew, Tim, Cameron Mackintosh and Robert Stigwood have done so much for musical theatre. They elevated the British musical and brought a lot of money into the country. The theatre industry makes a great deal of money for the UK and generates more than television or film.

In 1973 Tim and Andrew were honoured by the government for export earnings: £13 million for *Superstar*. And that was just the beginning of their success. *Superstar* just ran and ran. Bernard Delfont called it 'the musical *Mousetrap*' and when that first, long run finally ended in 1980 – after 3,358 performances – the curtain was down only for a moment. The show was immediately resurrected and went on a provincial tour of the UK. It has been revived ever since by many producers – including myself. Norman Jewison directed it as a movie in 1973 with Ted Neely as Jesus.

The film did not detract from the interest in theatrical productions which is always a fear for producers and writers. *Evita* is the only other Lloyd Webber work to be made into a film and that took until 1997 when Alan Parker turned Madonna into Eva Peron.

Jesus Christ Superstar has been translated into twenty-two languages and earned more than £100 million. It changed the world's view of theatre and it began the explosion that made London the epicentre of musical theatre.

Shows were being created to run, run, run. Not for months as in the past but for years. When it closed in the West End after eight years *Superstar* had overtaken *Oliver!*, *The Sound of Music*, *My Fair Lady*, *The Boy Friend*, *Fiddler on the Roof*, *Me and My Girl* and other more traditional shows as the longest-running musical in British theatre history.

I was glad to have been a part of that. I had been playing the leading part in a brand new musical that was the talk of the town. I was earning good money. I was not personally happy about what had happened with Susan but it had happened and I had found somebody that I was very much in love with. Linzi and I were beginning to build our lives together but always taking into account that I already had two children. They always came first.

Linzi and I had a lot of outgoings. Being in a hit show provided tremendous security for me and was the backbone of my existence for many years. This is why I believe in the theatre so much. More than 60 per cent of actors are out of work at any given time. For me, to be in a show that might run for a year meant financial security. If you can get into a show and earn regular money, that is about as secure as it gets.

People ask me, 'Don't you get bored doing the same thing every night?' The truth is that as an actor you change your job more often than most people change jobs. We can go to television or film or do other shows, if we are lucky.

After *Superstar* I needed another job.

6
Karma Chameleon

If I seem to be running, it's because I'm pursued.

— Mia Farrow, 1972

Linzi was in the cast of *Superstar* and was listed in the credits on the same line as Elaine Paige. At work she was helping me be *Jesus Christ Superstar*, but at home she was teaching me to be Jeeves. To tidy up after myself.

She taught me how to live with someone. Although I had been married I had never got around to learning the skills of co-habitating, of giving and taking in day-to-day life. My grandmother had picked up after me for years and Linzi was not about to do that. I got better.

We moved to a rented two-bedroom flat opposite the British Museum right in the heart of theatreland. We had a very good relationship and all the time I was learning to be more considerate, something I had never been before. I didn't know how to deal with people. Linzi had come from a very good home and her father and mother had taught her to be considerate and thoughtful. Sooner or later you have to throw away all the baggage. You have to be willing to change, to learn and move forward. You have to make a conscious decision to do it. Otherwise, you are going nowhere. Linzi helped me learn this lesson in life and it is an enormously important one.

I had a more ordered life and that meant I behaved in a

87

better way. I am not a conventionally religious person, but I believe in a certain amount of karma. That if you start behaving in a proper manner, better things will happen to you without you even realizing it. Our life as a couple improved and so did my career.

Much can be attributed to karma, to providence, but you still have to create the circumstances – the right career moves – that will allow it an environment in which to work. Some performers decide early on that if they cannot be a star, a leading man, they will give up. If you love to do it, I think you should stick with it, keep on trying. There are few people who make it overnight. Your time may be later in life. Nothing's wasted.

One of the good lessons I learned was playing a pair of boots in 1971. The film was a vehicle for Mia Farrow, who, after becoming a big star in television with *Peyton Place* and in film with *Rosemary's Baby*, was trying a different movie genre. In *Blind Terror* she was a blind girl being hunted by a psychopath at a country estate. It was an edge-of-the-seat thriller directed by Richard Fleischer who had worked with John Wayne, Orson Welles and many big names stretching as far back as Howard Hughes. My place in this roll of honour was 'The Boots'. I was the character in cowboy boots always trying to throttle Mia.

In the film all the audience saw of me were my feet. I wasn't called on to the film set by 'Mr Nicholas is needed' but 'Boots, come here.' It was a little bit degrading but I learned about how to hit my mark, about the film environment. I was getting lessons in acting and being paid at the same time. That was enough. I had and retain a thirst for knowledge, a desire to be better.

But even after *Hair, Superstar* and a couple of films, I felt I didn't know enough about acting. I was on the look-out for an opportunity all the time. I went to see shows, movies, revues – anything to help me learn. That was when nostalgia and *Grease* arrived. Jim Jacobs and Warren Casey wrote the lyrics and the music. It was set in 1950s America. All James Dean and tight angora sweaters.

It was also a big Broadway hit and a young Richard Gere – who was replaced in New York by John Travolta – was brought to London to star in the show. It went on at the New London Theatre in Drury Lane. I had gone along to auditions with my friend Andy Foray from *Hair*. He thought he stood a good chance, being American. I went to play the piano for him. While I was there I thought I would have a shot and audition myself. They ended up offering me the second lead to Richard, Kenickie. Andy didn't get a part. He said, 'Next time I'll play the piano.'

However, I wasn't interested in playing Kenickie. I wanted the lead, Danny, so I turned it down. When Richard left they asked me to take over. I jumped at the chance. Elaine Paige became Sandy and together we joined the show.

The first production of *Grease* was staged in a Chicago street-car station and lasted five hours. Two enterprising producers acquired the stage rights and Jim Jacobs and Warren Casey were brought in to provide the music, book and lyrics. It was first produced at the Eden Theater, New York on 14 February 1972 and moved to the Broadhurst Theater on 7 June 1972. *Grease* rode the nostalgia fad of the time and was a terrific hit. It outran *Fiddler on the Roof* and at one point was the Great White Way's longest running musical. It was Jacobs and Casey's only musical theatre success, but it was huge.

The love story of Sandy Dumbrowski and Danny Zuko was centred on sentimental memories of 1950s high school. Sandy and Danny meet at the beach and engage in a sweet romance. After a lot of acne and angst they end up together. I had seen the show in New York with Barry Bostwick playing the lead and had loved it. Now with Elaine Paige as Sandy, we took over the roles.

The interesting thing about *Grease* is that it never dates. It reflects so much of what it's like to grow up through those teenage years. We all know what it's like to feel soppy about a teenage romance. I can remember feeling so intensely about girls when I was thirteen. It's the same with kids of today. All this coupled with a funny script and a strong score means that *Grease* will still be packing them in a hundred years from now.

Grease was my third show and again proved a valuable learning experience for me. Danny is a real character. He's tough, vulnerable, funny and has to sing and dance. Apart from Herod's song, *Superstar* had no laughs. *Hair* had a few but this was a real comedy role. I began to enjoy that aspect more than any other. I learnt about timing a laugh and just what a delicate thing comedy is. It still fascinates me that if the line isn't timed perfectly the audience response won't be as good. Even the slightest move from a fellow performer or cough from a member of the audience can kill a laugh stone dead. I loved learning that skill. Some performers are lucky enough to have instinctive comic timing, others don't. I discovered that I did have a natural inclination for comedy, something that was to stand me in good stead later.

I suppose the difficulty for Elaine and myself was fitting into an existing company. When you're part of an original cast, a certain bonding takes place. Everyone gets very used to each other's delivery. New cast members are never quite the same. However, after a year of being crucified eight times a week, I was ready to have some fun.

Grease was a real eye opener. Elaine was a wonderful Sandy. Eva Peron, Edith Piaf and Norma Desmond in *Sunset* were to follow. We are very similar in that we both tend to be apprehensive about our capability to play a part. Yet, I have never seen a performance from Elaine where she didn't deliver. I think we both have a little more faith in ourselves now that we are older.

Grease was never deemed a hit. It opened at the newly built New London Theatre and it was generally believed that the public wasn't familiar with its location.

It could also have been the mood of the times. *Superstar* was still the big show along with *Godspell* starring David Essex as Jesus at Wyndhams. Most of the shows going into the West End were from America. The rock version of *The Two Gentlemen of Verona* had been huge in the States but there wasn't much support for it in London.

With *Grease* I do not think there was the power of nostalgia that existed in New York. Britain was more interested in *Oh! Calcutta!*. We were going forward rather than looking back. Nevertheless, we ran for nine months but did not achieve the status the production deserved. It was the wrong time for a good show.

It left me out of a job. How do you follow three major West End productions? A couple of old acquaintances – Jesus and Pete Townshend – helped out. As well as a director who enjoyed breaking the casting rules.

In 1973, David – now Lord – Puttnam had produced a film titled *That'll Be the Day*. It was written by the rock journalist Ray Connolly, and Keith Moon was involved as musical director as well as being in the film. It looked back at their earlier years, to 1958. The British cinema if not the theatre was into nostalgia.

David Essex played Jim Maclaine in what was a kitchen sink to pop star drama. There was quite a bit of realism in it with the added novelty attractions of Ringo Starr and the late Billy Fury in the cast. The story had Jim Maclaine leaving his family and drifting around in an attempt to be a pop star. It was a fun film, especially for people like me who were so aware of that world.

91

A year later much of the same team made a sequel called *Stardust*. This time I was in the cast with Adam Faith, Marty Wilde and Larry Hagman who would later become J.R. Ewing in *Dallas*. This time David's Jim Maclaine finds and loses fame. I played Johnny who is the leader of the Stray Cats group until David Essex turns up and takes over the group and I get kicked out.

It was a terrific experience for me. I enjoyed working with such familiar names and watching them, always learning. Hagman was a larger-than-life character even then. He was playing a brash American and you knew he was around on and off screen. He brightened up everyone's day.

I needed brightening up. I have always been a worrier and although everything was going well in the theatre and with the added attractions of film roles, I felt things were just not *right*. I felt I wasn't properly established in a particular area. I still didn't feel like a *real* actor. I was approaching my thirtieth birthday so maybe I was at that dangerous age. Frank Dunlop gave me more to worry about.

Frank had immense theatrical experience and an imaginative way about him. He was very open-minded about who he cast in his productions. One of his 'finds' was Jim Dale who had enjoyed a wide-ranging career. In the 1950s he had four pop record successes. In 1967 he won an Oscar for writing the lyrics for the theme song to the movie *Georgy Girl*, which starred Lynn Redgrave and Charlotte Rampling, and he was a regular in the *Carry On* films.

At first glance, not a candidate for the National Theatre or the Young Vic. That is not the way Frank Dunlop thinks. He cast Jim as Scapino and his acrobatic performance was wonderful. It took him to New York and on to international acclaim as a musical artist. Now, Frank wanted me for the part of Claudio in *Much Ado About Nothing*. For me it was a lot of to-do. I had never read a Shakespeare play, much less acted in one. I went out and bought this paperback copy of *Much Ado About Nothing*. An easy-reader edition. I went to see Frank and he said, 'Would you like to be Claudio?'

I replied, 'I don't think I can do it.'

'Of course, you can,' was his response.

'I don't know about this . . .'

'Rehearsals start in three weeks.'

And they did.

I started studying the text. I had seen *Hamlet* when I was about nine at The Old Vic. I was confused and didn't understand a word of it. My reaction was much the same when I began reading *Much Ado About Nothing*. The Shakespearean text was difficult and it took me about three weeks before I knew what I was talking about.

When I went for the first read-through everyone was very nice, very chummy. It was not the hippie world of *Hair* or the rock 'n' roll of *Grease*. This was the legitimate theatre, a Brave New World, a much more luvvie world. They were a totally different breed of people. I was surrounded by proper actors and had to read a play that I barely understood. The worst thing was having to read in front of them. It was frightening but I got through it. I didn't sound too bad.

Frank seemed pleased. He is very jolly and does not give a toss about anybody and loves a bit of aggravation. He likes to send the fighter planes in. I was flying one. The snobbishness that pervades so called 'legitimate' theatre was instantly apparent.

The musical performer is regarded by some 'proper' theatre types as in some way inferior. I do not believe it for a moment; for the most part that is nonsense. It takes as much skill to perform in a musical show as it does to play Shakespeare. Also, comedy is more difficult to do than drama. You're are either funny or you're not. In drama you can get away with it.

Frank, who is a legitimate theatre director – he ran the

Edinburgh Festival for some years – doesn't have any snob-
bery about him. His taste is eclectic. He directed Cliff Richard
in *Heathcliffe* which was horribly criticized. I went to see it
and I don't think it was the fault of the direction or of Cliff.
Ultimately, the piece was not quite good enough but Cliff
proved his popularity by selling thousands of seats. I am sure
Frank saw *Heathcliffe* as something new for his wonderful
imagination to take on. He's like that. He was very kind to me
because I wasn't an actor. I was still learning, so to be invited
to join the Young Vic Company was a huge honour.

There was one partiuclar actor in *Much Ado* who was very
resentful of what I was. He was very snooty. We were friends
in the play but off stage it got so bad that one night we both
snapped and ended up having a little dust up. The actors, on
stage, were waiting for us to make our entrance while we
were in the wings beating the crap out of each other. Finally
we were thrown on stage and became the great friends our
parts required. What acting!

Pete Townshend had my number and called me offering a
reading with Ken Russell who was being touted in the newspapers as 'the world's most successful director'. It was for a
role in Russell's film adaptation of the Who's rock opera
Tommy. Roger Daltrey had the title role and Ann-Margret,
Eric Clapton, Elton John and Tina Turner were also in the
cast.

I met Ken Russell in a studio in Battersea and he was so
enthusiastic. He wanted me to play nasty, 'orrible Cousin
Kevin who terrorizes poor, blind Tommy. I was thrilled. I sang
Cousin Kevin and although not a big part, it made quite an
impact. The late, great characters Oliver Reed and Keith
Moon were in the picture and there was a lot of rivalry
between them. The larger-than-life antics happened away
from the set. *Tommy* was an amazing movie with a sound-

track to match. It was a hip film for me to be associated with and rather good preparation for my own pop career.

Anger made me a pop star. And very famous. I was enjoying my success in the theatre and work in the movies. However, as always, I wanted to do more.

There is a need in most performers to be taken seriously. It's why Tony Hancock wanted to play Hamlet. Tommy Cooper did it for laughs on television but comics, like most entertainers, have thespian dreams. I would gladly have played Hamlet. I nearly did. I was to be cast as Hamlet in New York in a Broadway musical production.

In London, I had joined The Prospect Theatre Company which was a very worthy outfit run by Toby Robertson. They were involved in a musical version of John Bunyan's *Pilgrim's Progress* titled *Pilgrim*. Toby's wife, Jane McCulloch, was the librettist/lyricist. Paul Jones, the former Manfred Mann singer, was Christian, whom composer Carl Davis had confronting demons and temptations. Ben Cross, who co-starred in that Oscar bonanza *Chariots of Fire*, played Faithful. Peter Straker was a flaming Apollyon and Giant Despair. I had five parts including Mrs Giant Despair but the most fun was Mr Worldly Wiseman. I wore a bowler hat, red lip gloss and a jacket without a shirt. It was a strong cast and the music was sound but there was a lack of oomph about the production.

We were on tour with *Pilgrim* in Liverpool when I received a call from my agent: 'I've just had a call from America from a director called Gower Champion. They've seen you in *Tommy* playing Cousin Kevin. They want to fly you to New York to audition for a new musical called *Rockabye Hamlet*. They want you for the part of Hamlet. Will you audition?' he asked. 'Which way to Heathrow?' I replied.

I was given time off *Pilgrim* to fly to New York for Gower Champion. He was an American dancer/choreographer who had appeared with his sister Marge in 1950s movie musicals like *Mr Music* and *Show Boat* and was now a director. All that they had seen me do was drag poor Roger Daltrey of the Who around by his hair in *Tommy*. I was not going to argue. I auditioned and Gower said, 'We want you to play Hamlet. We want you to come back to America. We open in twelve weeks.'

I was released from *Pilgrim* so that I could begin rehearsals. There was just one snag. 'No, we don't have a work permit for you at this point but we don't see it as a problem.'

Then, as now, producers had to justify to the acting union – American Equity – that you were a name of such standing that you merited the part over an American actor. I had to organize my portfolio of credits and send it to the Department of Immigration who issued the work permits. I flew to America. I was on a tourist visa and living in a hotel room. I rehearsed with Gower every day and learned the music to his version of *Hamlet*. Every day they said the permit was in the post. The opening night deadline was fast approaching. The full cast had to rehearse and they still hadn't cleared their Hamlet with the US government.

I joined up with my old friend Paul Jabara in New York. He was very much into the gay scene. He loved Bette Midler and would regularly watch her sing at the baths in New York. She was a friend of his and we visited her apartment and had tea with her. Paul and I went to a bar called Reno Sweeneys to see her piano player cum musical director whose name was Barry Manilow. He was playing the piano and singing. I didn't know who he was but I couldn't believe how good his songs were. I thought they were classy. So much so, that we had a drink with Barry afterwards and I told him I made records and that I would like to record a couple of his songs. He gave me some demos and later I recorded one of them entitled 'I Am Your Child'. I still have the demos.

I met him again years later when I was performing panto

in Manchester. I was doing *Aladdin* with Eartha Kitt and Barry Manilow came to see the show. I was playing Aladdin and at the end of the panto I used to get the kids up on the stage to tell a joke. The audience knew Barry was in the theatre that night and one of the kids came up to tell his joke and it went like this: 'What time did Barry Manilow arrive at the theatre tonight?' 'I don't know. What time did Barry Manilow arrive at the theatre tonight?' I replied. All the audience were laughing because a lot of them could see Barry in the theatre. The kid said, 'Ten minutes after his nose.'

The kid had more success with his joke than I did on my trip to New York. This was to be my big break on Broadway. To play the lead in *Rockabye Hamlet*. I didn't get the permit and someone else played Hamlet and the show opened and closed within two weeks. I got no satisfaction from that.

I was severely pissed off. I was disillusioned when I arrived back in London. I wasn't famous enough to qualify for the work permit. I decided – no, I pledged – to become famous. I was determined. The theatre didn't reach enough people and with shows like *Hair* there was no individual billing. I had done only a little television and had no immediate contacts.

Music was the path. I would make records. Hit records. Fame was the game. I decided to try and have a hit record. To have a hit record, you need a good song and to find a good song, you need good writers. I had written a couple of songs and Chris Neil – who was my understudy in *Superstar* – co-produced the records with me. Chris has a great pair of 'ears' and his background was similar to mine.

I wrote a couple of songs with him and we recorded them for the RSO label. One was a song I had written called 'Shuffling Shoes'. It did not become a hit but it got enough radio play for RSO to allow me to make another record. I realized my own songs weren't good enough and I needed to find a hit elsewhere. An old friend from *Hair* called Johnny

Bergman told me of two songwriters called Dominic Bugatti and Frank Musker. They lived in two rooms on Prince Albert Road and I went to see them. They played me a lot of their songs but none of them sounded like a hit. As I was going out of the door I looked back and pleaded, 'Have you got anything else?'

They reluctantly put on a song called 'Reggae Like It Used to Be'. I think they were embarrassed to play it. I think they felt it was a little too bubblegum. I listened and after about thirty seconds I thought, 'That's it, that's the one.' I knew instantly. I had no doubt. It sang *hit*.

I took their backing track and played it to Chris Neil. He liked it too. So we went into a studio. I put my voice on the track and we added a saxophone and some violins. The writers sang harmony along with Chris. I took it to RSO Records and they released it.

What I didn't have was an image. I was no Gary Glitter. I remembered Mr Worldly Wiseman from *Pilgrim* and opted for a bowler hat and an open jacket with no shirt.

RSO got me a television show. I was booked on an afternoon pop show for kids. I was to sing 'Reggae Like It Used to Be' on the first day of the record's release. Unfortunately for me, the then Prime Minister – Harold Wilson – decided that it was time to call it a day. Wilson resigned! They cancelled the show. I was not pleased.

Luckily, a week is a long time in politics. Politicians go but TV shows go on for ever. 'Reggae Like It Used to Be' made Number 18 in the Top Twenty. It was one of the most thrilling moments of my life to have a record in the charts. I had fooled around with bands for most of my career and never got anywhere. Now at 30, I had found my hit. I became a pop star.

I was on *Top of the Pops* and I was achieving what I set out to do. I was marginally famous. DJs were playing Paul Nicholas and it was wonderful. Even more wonderful was that people were buying my records. I had a record in the charts. I loved it.

I wanted another song from Bugatti and Musker who were also performers. They wrote 'Dancing with the Captain'. They gave me a version to do and they did their own. We were competing against each other. They were competing against themselves, which was stupid.

To make a pop record you have to pay attention to detail. These were lightweight songs and you had to make them interesting. It was bubblegum music but there had to be something to chew. The trick is to make the song *live* for three minutes. It's not always easy, particularly with novelty songs. They were not substantial in themselves and needed a lot of dressing. Some work; some don't. It's always the basics that tell you. Unless the song presented to you on a piano in the front room excites you in some way, you can forget it. You have to like it instantly.

I have a good ear and I picked the songs. 'Dancing with the Captain' got into the Top Ten. At least we weren't one-hit wonders.

I was a pop star and I thought I should live like one. Linzi was at home and I was hanging around various clubs. I am not a drinker but I began to drink. I used to exaggerate my capacity in newspaper stories to boost my 'wild' image. The truth is, three lagers and I'm paralytic!

I was not behaving like someone who had the woman he loved waiting for him at home. What astonished me about this rock-star life was that this crowd drank all the time and then went to the gym and did circuit training. I didn't mind lifting a glass of lager, but I wasn't very good at lifting the weights. I was staying out until the early hours of the morning. I wasn't paying Linzi much attention and she was getting more and more fed up.

But someone, somewhere, was sticking pins in my doll.

Voodoo? I don't know. Chris Neil is a terrific record producer and he said to me one day, 'You've done two really good poppy songs. You should do a ballad. I have this great idea for an arrangement of "If You Were the Only Girl in the World".' The song was a ballad from way back.

I agreed. That voodoo doll was working. He produced a great version, not unlike 10cc's 'I'm Not in Love'. There were lots of overlays of voices singing harmonies and technically it was brilliantly made. The public didn't go for it. No one was remotely interested. What Chris had tried to do was give me more credibility with a classier record but unfortunately no one wanted to buy it.

It was released, got a few plays and then it died. We had tried to change my direction after only two hits. There's nothing wrong with that except that the song that we chose wasn't right for me.

Britain loves Christmas songs. There are always a handful vying for the top spot. Mine was 'Grandma's Party' and there was no question in my mind that it would be a hit. It was lightweight but it was very catchy. It was well produced and waltzed into the Top Ten. Everyone, for a very short time, wanted to be at 'Grandma's Party'.

Whereas that single was a gimmick song, the next one, 'Heaven on the Seventh Floor', was cute to the nth degree and as irresistible as every cuddly toy in the shop. The record was perfect for the American market and was released there. It went to Number 5 in the Billboard Top Hundred, giving me a gold disc for selling two million records. It was about a guy who got stuck in a lift with a beautiful girl and they fall in love.

My own love life was perishing at that point. Emotionally, my life was going in the opposite direction from my record career – with a bullet. Linzi wanted to fire one straight through my heart. She was fed up, not happy with the way I

was behaving. She saw me not as a wild rock 'n' roll star –
more like a right selfish sod!

It was a matter of respect. I wasn't giving her enough. I was
too busy getting on with my own life. It was a reflection of my
past, of a lifestyle I had grown up being an eyewitness too. I
was not as attentive as I should have been. I was not very nice
generally. She'd had enough. She wanted out. She wanted to
leave. And, much to my great chagrin, she did. I thought it
was just a tantrum. I should have known better. I had known
and loved Linzi for seven years. She doesn't do tantrums. She
acts on what she believes. She was convinced she and I had no
future. She had made a big improvement in me but I was still
not easy to live with. So she left.

Sometimes the ambition to achieve blinds you to what you
should conserve. Linzi elected to make a stand. She was off-
limits to me. She was a no-go area for Paul Nicholas. I felt
sorry for myself. Very sorry. I was alone in a flat, in an environment that had been created by this other person whom I
loved – but not enough to make sure she was happy too. I
constantly called Linzi and my message was always the same:
'Why don't you come back? I want you to come back.'

She did the opposite and began negotiating to buy her own
flat. I kept calling but she was stubborn, oblivious to anything
and everything I said. I was in limbo, lost. I had three hit
records in the UK and I was all over the magazines. I was 30
years old and had, in my terms at the time, made it. Susan
was getting on with her life. The kids were prospering at
school. Linzi had seriously given our relationship the elbow. It
was over, finished, as far as she was concerned, despite my
calls and, what I considered to be, my immense charm.

I was living the pop star life and staying out all night, for
I had no one and nothing to go home to. I'd never met anyone
who could rival Linzi. I was doing the club scene and generally misbehaving, waking up miserable in the wrong beds. I

don't know what I was trying to prove to myself or get out of my system. It was a crazy time. I behaved like someone I have never wanted to be. Professionally, my profile was going higher and higher. Granada Television had given me my own afternoon show called *Paul* which ran for two seasons. It was a successful kids afternoon pop show and I sang three or four songs and had guest stars every week. I was digging myself into the pop music world more and more deeply.

The pop business was not as fulfilling as I had hoped. The writers wanted to do stronger rock material but the music I was selling was on personality, on affability, songs to sing along with, not rock 'n' roll to. I was never a rock singer. I do not have the equipment, the natural facility of a Phil Collins or a distinctive enough voice to be able to do it. What turned me on in pop was the business of producing the records. I enjoyed the television appearances and the European promotional trips, but it was not that satisfying. It would have been when I was 17 but not at 30. The interesting part for me was picking the right song and getting it produced properly in the studio. I didn't like just being a singer. It had given me a much higher profile but it wasn't satisfying.

At this time I got a call from Ken Russell, the *enfant terrible* of the cinema with movies like *Women in Love* starring the late Oliver Reed and Alan Bates, as well as the controversial film *The Devils* with Reed and Vanessa Redgrave. Before *Tommy* he had made a film of the composer Mahler and now it was the turn of Wagner and Liszt.

Roger Daltrey had been cast as Liszt. This was Ken's interpretation on the life of the brilliant Hungarian pianist and composer Franz Liszt. Born in 1811, Liszt was a child prodigy who later went on to compose 'The Preludes', 'Orpheus', 'Hamlet' and 'Liebestraum' amongst others. He became a huge star and was fêted throughout Europe. I was cast as

Richard Wagner. Wagner was a prolific German composer born in 1813 who wrote 'The Flying Dutchman', 'The Ring' and 'Parsifal'. He was Hitler's favourite composer. A point not missed by Ken and clearly reflected in the film. After Wagner's first wife died, he married Liszt's daughter Cosima.

The film was Ken's usual mix of mad surrealism with Wagner cast as the villain. At one point Wagner turns into Dracula, sinking his teeth into Liszt's neck, suggesting that Wagner had stolen musical ideas from Liszt. In another scene Wagner becomes a cross between Frankenstein's Monster and Adolf Hitler.

The climax of the film is when 'the Abbé Liszt', who has now taken minor orders in the Roman Catholic Church, sets about exorcising the devil from the evil Wagner. The scene required me to fly around a room attached to a wire. It was technically quite difficult to shoot and took a long time to set up, which meant that we couldn't get many attempts at it. Everything was going beautifully: I was attached to the wire and was flying around the room about seven feet off the ground. Suddenly, the wire snapped. I crashed to the ground and thought for a moment that I had really injured myself. Luckily, I had only broken my ankle. I was quite brave in those days and didn't make too much fuss. I felt confident that we'd completed the shot. Ken was very kind and attentive. Then he said, 'Thank you. That was very good but we didn't quite get it. Would you mind doing it again?' Being young and keen I said, 'Of course Ken,' trying to ignore the excruciating pain in my right ankle. So I did it again with a broken ankle.

When I watched the film after its completion, I noticed that in the second half of the movie I am walking around with an unnaturally large right foot. This was because they had had to draw a huge mock shoe over my plaster cast to enable me to finish the film. It disguised nothing. Ken was great fun to work with and made every day exciting. I feel very privileged to have worked with such a creative director.

Despite parts such as this I was still a pop star who acted, who had theatrical knowledge and experience. I was in a void. And I was living alone for the first time in my life. What I did have were contacts and friends from *Hair* and *Superstar*. They were my Alma Mater. During the *Hair* tour I worked with an actor called Richard O'Brien. Some people thought he was a little strange but I put him down as intense. I saw potential in him. He had a quick, creative mind. What fascinated me was that when the others would take off for dinner or the pub, Richard would go off to write a musical. He played a couple of the numbers he had created and I was impressed. I went into a studio and recorded two of his songs. Richard was already working on *The Rocky Horror Show* and the two songs later appeared in the show. I introduced Richard to Jim Sharman and later they worked together on a production of Sam Shepard's *The Unseen Hand* at the Royal Court Theatre in London. That was before they put together *The Rocky Horror Show*, which remains one of the great camp takes on horrid Hollywood horror movies. The legend of *Rocky Horror* and its stars, like Tim Curry, began in the small Theatre Upstairs at the Royal Court in 1973.

My enthusiasm for Richard's idea and music came back to me – maybe it was karma working once more – when three years later he took *T. Zee* to the Royal Court. This time, because of the economics of the success of *Rocky Horror*, he was given the main stage to present his show.

The premise was two explorers, played by Richard and Belinda Sinclair, entering into a fantastic Hollywood underworld of sexual shenanigans, ruled over by a dreadful despot called Bone Idol. That was me.

Warren Clarke, who would become so popular in the *Dalziel and Pascoe* series, was a fat Tarzan who roamed around the audience looking for his Jane. Diane Langton was a *Star Wars* type as Princess La and her motivation was that she couldn't get enough sex. So, just being a sadistic pop manipulator was quite an uplifting role for me. The show ran its course at the Royal Court but it never had the cult status of *Rocky Horror*. There was nothing new to say. The times were changing and, tragically for me and my family, beyond the stage, in the real world.

7
Tragedy

Just Tell Me When To Cry.

*– autobiography of Richard Fleischer,
director of* The Jazz Singer.

I was very much taken with acting and intrigued by film. One miserable February afternoon Louis Caballero, who had been in *Hair* with me, turned up at the flat and suggested we go and see Mel Brooks's comedy *Silent Movie*. Brooks had the wild idea of making a film without sound. One of the better jokes in the film is when the mime artist Marcel Marceau speaks the only word in the entire movie which is 'Non'. The film was just OK and I trudged home on my own in the rain.

I was shaken out my thoughts by a phone call from my mother. I could hear she was terribly upset. She could hardly get the words out. She managed to tell me that there had been an accident but was too upset to go into detail. They talk about 'numb with shock' and that is exactly how she sounded. I kept asking, 'Are the kids OK?' She managed to answer, 'Yes, yes.' It took another phone call from me to discover that Susan had died in the accident. In a car crash.

Susan had let out a couple of rooms and John – one of the lodgers – explained what had happened. I had met him and Ron, a younger lad who was also lodging at Susan's. John was very calm and clear with his news. Susan, who was 28, had been killed outright in the crash. Ron who was only 19, had been in the car with her and had also died.

I was in shock, in a complete daze. I got a cab. I don't know why I didn't drive myself – I usually do. But the cab took me to Susan's house in Elstree. My mother was already there. She told me what had happened. Susan and Ron had gone for a lunchtime drink. They had not had an excessive amount and Susan had let Ron drive them home.

They were only about two hundred yards from the pub *en route* to Elstree. The road that they were driving on has a terribly sharp bend. I knew from my own experience how severe it was. Going around the bend Ron had lost control and hit another car head on and Susan and Ron were killed instantly. The occupants of the other car, although badly hurt, thankfully later recovered.

My mother was obviously in a terrible state. After school, Natasha, who was ten, and Oscar, who was eight, had been picked up by Susan's friend and taken to her house. She didn't tell them what had happened.

A young policeman arrived at Susan's house and filled me in on the details. It was straightforward, part of their training, and as sensitively done as anything can be in such circumstances. The horror of it became real, I knew it was true, so awful and true. One moment someone's there and then they're not. Nothing so shocking had ever happened to me before.

I had watched my grandad Oscar die of cancer but it was a gradual process. He would go into remission and look better and I would think, 'He's going to be all right.' I thought he was strong and would survive but when he eventually died, we were prepared. With Susan it was instant. All my thoughts were with Susan and then it hit me. The kids! Ten and eight years old. I knew I had to be strong for them, for Oscar and Natasha. It sounds a terrible cliché but it is at times of extreme shock that we think that way.

I went round to get them that evening to tell them what

had happened. There was no point in trying to disguise what the reality of it was, or trying to talk around it. I had to tell them that their mum had died. I told them in the bedroom of Susan's friend's house. I did not want to wait until I got back to their home because they could see by the look on my face that something was terribly wrong. I tried to cushion it without thinking about the words. They had known something was wrong. Susan had not collected them from school. They were at another person's house until 8 p.m. Where was Mum? It was the most difficult thing I have ever had to do in my life. I told them roughly what had happened and that their mummy had gone to heaven. I did not know what else to tell them. Two little kids looking into my eyes, trying to understand. You do it. I was in shock as well. When I told them what had happened, they cried instantly. They just both wept and wept.

Then we got to Susan's house. Her presence was everywhere. It was so dreadful to see her things. All the reminders of her. I was completely devastated. It made me realize that nothing else in this world is as important as the people you love or care for. We were divorced but I still loved her. She was the mother of our kids. Our marriage had not worked out and I'd resolved to try and do the best I could for her and the kids. But I was totally unprepared for what had happened.

My mother was a rock. I needed support and there was only one person I could turn to. I turned to Linzi. I had not seen her for nine months. She was still in the cast of *Superstar* and I called her after work and explained what had happened to Susan. She didn't say much. She too was in shock. She just drove to be with me and the kids. Our main concern was for the children.

Linzi arrived and helped me from then on. Nothing was said or communicated in words. We put the kids to bed and managed to get them off to sleep. I couldn't sleep. Linzi and I

111

talked for most of the night. It was a great comfort to me that she was there.

It wasn't easy for her, yet it had seemed the most natural thing for me to call her and ask her to come and help because I was finding it difficult to come to terms with the whole thing. It was the loss of Susan. The actual physical loss. The realization that you cannot ever bring that person back. You're powerless to do anything.

Thank God I had the practical back up of my mother and Linzi. I didn't want to uproot the kids and Linzi and my mum were there to help me on a day-to-day level. The children were able to stay in the same house and remain at the same school. The long-term plan was for us all to live together. The kids, Mum and Linzi.

I did not want to throw away any of Susan's things. You quickly realize that memories and a few possessions are all that you have left when someone dies. On the day of the funeral, I didn't want to take Natasha and Oscar to the cremation service. I didn't want them to have to endure it. So afterwards we went to their local church and had a special service for them.

We all gathered at Susan's house. For those intimately involved these are such surreal occasions. People were drinking and laughing. It seemed to me to be a terrible thing to do when you have just lost someone you deeply love. I thought that was wrong. I don't feel like that now. I realize it is a necessary part of letting go. It was good for people to be able to talk about her and unwind from what, for everyone, had been an emotional, horrible day.

Susan was a lovely, bubbly person and so full of life. She had everything to look forward to. We were not together but we were friends and we shared our love for Oscar and Natasha. For me there was the guilt of not being around during their formative years. I was the father who left and then returned but I returned without their mum. It's been difficult for all of us. We have never really discussed Susan's death. It was always too painful.

Linzi was marvellous with them. She was someone they already knew. She did not try and take on the role of their mother. Linzi was my friend. She was helping me to look after them. We had taken them out together for at least six years and as far as they were concerned, she wasn't a stranger. She was never referred to as Mum. They always called her Linzi.

I hope I was there to give them what I had always tried to give them, the love of a father. I wanted the best for them in terms of education, accommodation and opportunity. It is all a parent can do for his or her children. I think children are a law unto themselves and you can affect them but they contrive their own destinies. Oscar went into the film business – he worked on movies like *Four Weddings and a Funeral* – and in 1999 formed his own production company. Natasha has three beautiful children of her own, Ruby, Joseph and Amber. She is a qualified psychiatric nurse and helps kids with special needs. What happened to Susan has shaped all our lives. I know she would be proud of what the children have made of themselves.

With hindsight, it is sad that so much hurt is engendered when a marriage breaks up. There is so much pressure on people in modern society to have fun. There are so many temptations. Marriage – like most things in life – seems to be quite disposable. You have to work at it. Nothing is perfect. It's all about compromise.

Linzi and I have been together for thirty years and we've had our ups and downs. Linzi is a very good person and I have been very lucky to have found her. She has done a great deal for me. If I had not found such a wonderful person, my life would have been very different. My attraction to Linzi has always been her honesty. She is genuine and she has never let me down. When I first got to know her, I knew I had found someone special. Someone I could rely on. Most of all she helped me rebuild the family and create a home for us all. That is the most precious gift anyone could ever receive.

I have not said very much about Ron who died alongside Susan on that terrible day. At times of great tragedy, we can become immersed in our own grief. It was as great a loss for Ron's family as it was for ours. Our families will always share the memory of two loved ones, who will remain for ever in our hearts.

8

Frankie and I go to Hollywood

You can't find true affection in Hollywood because
everyone does the fake affection so well.

– Carrie Fisher, 1979

P op music was getting into a rut and professionally I felt the same. The punk movement shook it up with Johnny Rotten as the flip side of Paul McCartney. The safety pins and torn T-shirts were an antidote to songs like 'Dancing with the Captain'. I have never objected to 'Never Mind the Bollocks' as an anthem. But the world and most of all America still enjoyed a cuddle with their entertainment. And there was never a cuddlier song than 'Heaven on the Seventh Floor'. When it was released in the States I went there to promote it.

In 1978 the talk shows dominated afternoon and late-night television. Johnny Carson was a god and there were several others who were admired by the critics, like Michael Parkinson, with audiences running into zillions. I was perfect for them – this harmless, cute, blond-haired British singer with this unthreatening record. American television producers had pushed the pause button on punk. I was a delight for them. I was on *The Dinah Shore Show* (her boyfriend was Burt Reynolds who was then the biggest movie star in the world) and *The Mike Douglas Show* and *The Merv Griffin Show*.

With the help of that nationwide exposure 'Heaven on the Seventh Floor' was steaming up the US charts and suddenly this record was Number 5 on the Billboard Top Hundred.

117

I was a star – a pop star. At the same time my friend Paul Jabara, from *Superstar* and the 10 Downing Street railings, was enjoying a huge career. He had written a song for a movie called *Thank God It's Friday* which was all about the problems at a Hollywood discotheque. The cast was not well known and the movie never was either. But Paul's song 'Let's Dance' was a disco anthem and sung by Donna Summer who had been on the German tour of *Hair* with Linzi. He won an Oscar for Best Original Song. He always said it was the best nine inches he'd ever received.

That connection – and they are so important – led him to write 'No More Tears (Enough is Enough)' which was a Number 1 hit in America for what was a dream team, Barbra Streisand and Donna Summer. He wrote it for Streisand's movie *The Main Event* at her invitation. He told me, 'On the way over to Streisand's house to talk about the film I was a wreck. I couldn't believe I was writing a song for *her*. The only thing wrong with the song was that with Barbra and Donna there was not a singing part for me.'

It was a joy to be with Paul and see what success could be achieved. When I returned to Britain, I came back a pop star – and went back almost by return to Hollywood for a movie.

It was not *Gone with the Wind* but it was a lavish Tinseltown production of *Sergeant Pepper's Lonely Hearts Club Band* which was produced by Universal Studios and the Robert Stigwood organization. A loose storyline had been created around the Beatles' classic, best-known album. Peter Frampton was a big, big star at the time and he starred as Billy Shears and I was his brother Dougie Shears, the manager of the Band which also comprised the Bee Gees – Barry, Maurice and Robin Gibb. The late, lovely Frankie Howerd was the villain, 'Mean Mr Mustard', who appeared in the Beatles' *Abbey Road* Album. Frankie and I had gone to

Hollywood at the same time for the movie, which had an astonishing cast. There was the almost unknown Steve Martin, Donald Pleasence and, topping it off, Alice Cooper, Earth, Wind and Fire, and Aerosmith.

The tremendous bonus for me was working with George Burns, who even then was getting on: he was 82. He was helpful and nice to me. And wryly amusing. During filming, Bing Crosby died and the obituaries in the *Los Angeles Times* and the *Los Angeles Herald Examiner* both reported Crosby's age as 73. George looked up from the paper. 'Bing always lied about his age. He was 77. I watch these things. Got to keep an eye over your shoulder in this business.'

Another thrill of the film was 'covering' the famous Beatles songs on a soundtrack produced by George Martin who had been there for the original *Sergeant Pepper*. The Beatles graduated from writing good pop songs to the kind of music they played on *Sergeant Pepper*, which was truly fantastic. I think George Martin producing over-awed me more than attempting to do justice to the songs. I was in Hollywood for four months. It was a big production but a slow process. It was great to do a Hollywood movie and I also learned first hand how quick and fickle the pop business is.

Peter Frampton went into the movie as some sort of pop deity but by the end of filming it was the Bee Gees who were the stars, the gods. Although they were in *Sergeant Pepper* they were releasing songs like 'How Deep is Your Love?' and 'Jive Talking' and having enormous success. It was a big disco time.

It was fun to be there and also an escape from what had happened so recently in England. I was filming during Christmas and Linzi flew out with Natasha and Oscar. It was our first family Christmas. Mum seemed to go everywhere with me. She had been so wonderful during the crisis, it was nice to able to see her enjoy all the Californian sunshine. She went crazy in the giant supermarkets and the kids loved the restaurants, all those giant portions.

Being in California was an artificial release for all of us from the horror of Susan's death. I still had to find a home in Britain for all of us. Professionally, I was getting irritated by not being able to break away in acting from the pop-singer image. Of course, I did look the part.

And I wanted to work. So there I was rolling around in the back of a Rolls-Royce with the original Hollywood 'Baby Doll', Carroll Baker. She had followed that censorship-breaking classic working with James Dean in *Giant* and Alan Ladd in *The Carpetbaggers* and now here I was lusting with her, some many years later, in the Roller.

The film was *The World is Full of Married Men* and it was something of a morality tale by Jackie Collins but with all the sexy sequences intact. Tony Franciosa was Carroll's philandering husband and she was taking revenge by having sex with willing lads like me. I paid the price – I got shot at the end of the film.

It did not stop me being enchanted by Jackie Collins. She is great mates with Ian McShane and in the pre-*Lovejoy* days wrote a film for him titled *Yesterday's Hero* in which he played a George Best sort of character. The love interest was the American actress Suzanne Somers who was a big TV star in the States in *Three's Company*, which was the Hollywood version of *Man About the House*.

Adam Faith was in it as well and I played an Elton John character – a pop star who runs a football club. In movies I was most certainly being pigeonholed as a pop star who acted. I was playing third leads in those kind of films because of it. But no matter how frustrating it could be the money was nice. I could never deny that. And royalties were coming in from the records. Whatever I was doing in my career, at the back of my mind was always the security of the family. Financial risk was never an option. Linzi and I were seriously looking for a house. We looked in Hertfordshire near where the children had been living but decided we could accept only so much Green Belt in our lives.

We had lived in Muswell Hill and we were looking around that area when we saw this Georgian house in Highgate with a 'For Sale' sign out front. I liked the look of it. The driveway down at the side of the house was very rough but the main gate was open and we wandered down and beyond the garages. There was a huge garden and a coach house. I thought they were separate dwellings but the estate agent said it was all part of the same property. The house was run down, in a dreadful state. It was also under offer.

I thought that I had to have it. I got it within three days. I outbid the other people. I had made quite a lot of money for myself in those days, more than £300,000 just on pop singing. A fair whack from a few hit records. The only problem was in order to pay for the house and not to lose all the money to the taxman, I had to become a tax exile.

I was in a dilemma. What should I do? Do I get a nice house, give the kids a secure home, give us all a nice place to live or stay in Britain? I talked it over with Linzi and we decided there was no choice. I had to leave the country for a year. I had to do a year 'out' to save the money that I had made from pop singing.

The accountants had been very clear. If you stay you pay 98 per cent in the pound; if you go you don't. I have always joked that I was the only tax exile to go 'out' for £5,000. The truth is it was to save about £300,000. It was not Elvis Presley money but to a bloke like me who'd never had so much money in his life and who wanted to create something special for his family, it was, of course, a small fortune.

We sold the house in Elstree and the children, my mother, Linzi and I moved into our lovely Highgate home. My deadline for leaving England was 4 April, 1979. So if I was going to qualify for the 'year out', I had to leave before that date. After we had got back together, Linzi and I decided to have a baby and, two weeks prior to my leaving, it was confirmed that Linzi was pregnant. We were overjoyed, while at the same time worried that we were going to be apart for such a long period.

I decided to find a house in Los Angeles that would be big enough for the kids, Linzi and my mother to visit whenever school holidays permitted. I rented a nice house off Benedict Canyon, which is not a bad place to live, even by Hollywood standards. The only other option was to go and live in France but I didn't speak the language and I was never going to get any work there. I had a chance of being employed in Hollywood. My contacts were limited to Paul Jabara and Marsha Hunt. I rented a room from Marsha until I found my own place. It took me three months to get a Hollywood agent – there are plenty of actors in Hollywood. Everyone is an actor, be they waiter or petrol-pump attendant. Everyone is 'resting between acting jobs', so getting an American agent was something of a mini-triumph.

I got a guest spot on the Californian Highway Patrol series *Chips* with Erik Estrada and then – irony of irony – I was cast as a pop singer. An English punk, which I was not. But I had the right haircut and spoke with a London accent so I was a punk, a Johnny Rotten-type, as far as the Hollywood casting agents were concerned. It is similar to when they put English characters in US sitcoms such as *Friends* or *Frasier*: they cast what they think it should be, not what the reality is. It was a small part in a big movie. It was a remake of *The Jazz Singer* and the star was Neil Diamond making his acting début and the other big name was Laurence Olivier.

It was a troubled production and Richard Fleischer who had directed my feet in *Blind Terror* with Mia Farrow was

As that nasty Cousin Kevin in Ken Russell's madcap, wonderful classic *Tommy*. *(Top left)*

Wagner helps himself to a drop of Liszt's (Roger Daltrey) musical genius in Ken Russell's surreal *Lisztomania*. *(Top right)*

Elaine Paige and I, as Sandy and Danny, in the original London production of *Grease*. *(Centre)*

I'm the outsider of the 'Stray Cats', in the movie *Stardust*, looking moodily over at David Essex, Keith Moon, Dave Edmunds and Karl Howman. *(Above)*

With the kids.
Natasha aged ten,
Oscar aged eight,

Our first family
portrait after my
year's exile in
America. April
1980. (Left to
right: Natasha,
Alexander, me,
Oscar and Linzi.)

'After you.' Linzi and
I formally becoming
Mr and Mrs in 1984.

With the Bee Gees, while filming *Sergeant Pepper* in Los
Angeles. *(Above)*

The bowler-hatted pop singer – *Top of the Pops*, 1976. *(Right)*

Receiving a gold disc from the President of RSO records, Al
Coury (far right), for selling over a million copies of 'Heaven
on the Seventh Floor' in America. *(Below)*

The cat's whiskers. As Rum Tum Tugger in *Cats*. *(Top and above)*

Celebrating the beginning of the *Cats* phenomenon with Cameron Mackintosh. *(Above right)*

We knew we had a winner. Toasting *Cats* with Elaine Paige and Andrew Lloyd Webber. *(Right)*

The Pirate King in the *Pirates of Penzance*. A role that I have played many times. *(Above)*

Living a Dream: dancing with Cyd Charisse in *Charlie Girl*. *(Left)*

Blondel with the Blondettes. Tim Rice and Stephen Oliver's humorous musical about the medieval minstrel Blondel. *(Below)*

Just Good Friends. Jan Francis and I hit it off from the start – we shared a similar sense of humour.

Team-work. We worked hard to make the lines as natural as possible and it worked with the audiences: 22 million people viewed our Christmas special.

Director Joseph Brooks looks on anxiously as his wife Susan and I prepare for a big screen kiss in the film *Invitation to the Wedding*.

With Sir John Gielgud, who's giving me a talking to in his quaint American accent (*Invitation to the Wedding*).

Meeting Princes
Diana at the
Royal Gala.
I complimented
her on her
beautiful tan.
She replied,
'The sun always
shines on the
righteous.' (Abo

Meeting the Queen at the Royal
Command Performance with
Michael Ball and Rosemary
Ford. (Above)

High-powered Oscar: my father
introducing my former agent
Jan Kennedy to Lord Grade and
his wife. (Right)

brought in to take over the production. Richard told the story of Olivier wandering around the Goldwyn Studios looking for the set of *The Jazz Singer*, when a production girl encountered him and handed him a page and a half of new dialogue. Olivier read it and his remark became part of Hollywood legend, 'You know? This piss is shit.'

Luckily, my involvement in the movie did not involve too much angst on that level. I had to sing a number titled 'Love on the Rocks' – which would be a big hit song – as a punk. The scene involved Neil coming in and saying, 'No, it should be sung like this.' He then does his marvellous version of 'Love on the Rocks'. In character, I have a sarcastic look on my face and clap my hands mirthlessly and tell him: 'Piss off.' Which is as close to an Olivier line I think I have achieved.

I did learn that you *can* work in Hollywood. I was not known as an actor there at all but as a singer, but I proved the point. British actors in the year 2000 have a much better chance but I think, as in everything else, it requires dedication and perseverance. You have to have staying power.

All I wanted to do was get home. Alexander was born on 8 November 1979 but I didn't see him until he was about six weeks old, around Christmas time. We had not wanted to uproot Oscar and Natasha and bring everybody out because of school. So this was the first chance to see my new son. It was a very Hollywood event. I was at Los Angeles Airport to meet Linzi, my mother, Oscar, Natasha and my baby son Alexander.

Joan Collins had made something of a stir with a movie titled *The Bitch* and she was arriving at the same time. The publicity people had banners out reading: WELCOME THE BITCH. I was oblivious to this. My legs were like jelly waiting to see Alexander. When they came off the plane I did not know who to hug first. Mother or child? I found it easy to wrap my arms around both of them.

Then, I had Alexander in my arms and Joan Collins walked past and recognized me. She looked at this little bundle in my arms and said, 'Tut, tut, you naughty boy.'

Somehow, with all the excitement, I drove everybody back to the house and I felt so overwhelmed at seeing the family after so long. I hadn't seen them for three months. I was so excited I walked into the swimming pool. I was fully clothed and it was lucky I didn't have Alexander in my arms. I had just walked straight into the pool.

I made a little film of us that year. We all performed in it and we called it *The Blob from Outer Space*. Alexander was the blob. It was about a Martian who gets lost on earth. The children find him under the Christmas tree. Oscar and Natasha acted their parts beautifully and Alexander was the blob that they found under the tree. I was the dad from outer space who came to find the blob and take him home.

It was a real family time and wonderful. I saw the last few months of tax exile out knowing things would be good. Everybody, including my new son, was living in Highgate and *all* the children seemed as happy as they could be.

I had finished with pop singing. I had made a bit of money. We all had a decent place to live and I was on my way home. The accountants advised that I leave it a couple of weeks after the deadline of 5 April. I flew home on 6 April 1980.

It was a new beginning. I arrived back and for the first time was living with Oscar, Natasha, Alexander, Linzi, and my mum in a lovely house and that was how I wanted us to continue.

My career might have been a problem had the 1980s not found me in the most successful piece of musical theatre of all time – and the star of Britain's favourite situation comedy.

9

A Purr-fect Life

There is no limit to what cats can do with their
bodies.

– Gillian Lynne, 1980

There was no band playing, red carpet or any job offers when I first returned to Britain from California. Out of sight, out of mind. Or so I thought.

My year in America had provided the money for a lovely house, but there wasn't a lot left over after living away from home for a year. I needed to work. I looked around but I didn't want to be drawn back into the pop business. I had done that for four years and that is a long time in pop. I had done it to make a name for myself. That was very important to me. The one thing you want to be if you are a performer is famous. Warren Clarke once told how he got into the back of a cab and the driver said, 'What do you do?' Warren said, 'I'm an actor.' Warren had always had a small wart on the end of his nose. The driver looked closely at him and said, 'You won't get very far with that thing on the end of your conk!' Warren proved him wrong.

You are only as good as your last appearance. Mine was seven thousand miles away. The horrible thing about fame is that if you have done many different things, as I have, people get confused. Are you a pop singer, are you a musical performer, are you a sitcom actor or do you have the potential to do slightly more serious work? We all want to be big

Hollywood stars and do the very highest quality work but sometimes you have to take what you can get.

My motto has always been that this business is a marathon, not a sprint, and some artists have to do it for themselves and some get it given to them. Much like life. It is the luck of the draw. You only have to do one decent movie and you can live off it for the next ten years.

I was lucky enough to get a television play titled *A Little Roccoco* with Judy Cornwall in which I played an antique dealer. It was a romantic comedy. It was about a young man falling in love with an older woman. Of all the millions of people who watched it, one proved to be very important – John Sullivan, the creator and writer of *Just Good Friends*. That was unknown to me at the time and after the play I spent a lot of time twiddling my thumbs and worrying. The performer's lot is not an easy one.

Then out of nowhere I got a call from Andrew Lloyd Webber.

'Hello Paul. How are you?' he asked.

'I'm fine,' I said.

'Have you ever read *Old Possum's Book of Practical Cats* by T. S. Eliot?'

I said, 'Yes, it's standard reading for Kentish Town Secondary Modern.'

He said, 'Well, I'm doing it and I'd like you to be in it.'

That's how I became involved with *Cats*, the theatre's greatest commercial success.

Andrew has a church in his back garden at Sydmonton Court in *Watership Down* country. He said he was doing a workshop of *Cats* and could I be there to work with Gemma Craven and Gary Bond for the music festival he has at Sydmonton every summer. Before he put the phone down he said, 'I will send you a tape.'

I was thinking *Mission Impossible* and wondered if it would self-destruct after being played. The tape duly arrived of

Andrew playing the piano and singing the original score of *Cats*. I have saved it for posterity.

I went to his house in Eaton Square in London and he played me some more of the show and I was quite taken with it but I thought, 'Hang on. There is no story. This is a collection of poems, whimsical cat tales, and Andrew has put some nice tunes to them but I haven't heard a hit.' On consideration, as Andrew was the one with the church in his back garden and a large house in Eaton Square, I thought, 'Who am I to judge?'

I took off for Sydmonton Court to rehearse with Gary and Gemma and we spent the weekend working. The great thing about the upper classes is that they never seem to get cold. They never have the heating on. I was in a very draughty bedroom upstairs. Andrew was very hospitable but I froze.

We rehearsed on the Friday and performed the workshop of *Cats* the following evening. We had no idea this was the genesis of a show that would go around the world in ten translations and then go around again and again. It was the first British musical to play in Moscow. It has been seen by more than fifty million people.

But that evening in Andrew's back garden, the performance of T. S. Eliot's poems to Andrew's music was much appreciated by the small audience but especially by Valerie Eliot, the widow and former secretary of T. S. Eliot. Andrew knew he had something and, from that small workshop, he formed the idea of staging *Cats* as a full-scale musical.

Andrew's and Tim Rice's partnership had broken up and Andrew had not renewed his contract with Robert Stigwood. The contract Stigwood had bought out from David Land and Sefton Myers. Andrew now had control of his financial as well as his artistic freedom. He still had to find around £400,000 to stage *Cats*.

No one seemed especially interested in a show about cats.

What they didn't understand was that Andrew was creating an entertainment – a dance with wonderful music – that would travel. There were no boundaries, no borders, to music and dance. It would play as well in Tokyo as in Torquay. This was the beginning of the modern musical, the international production with the world's theatres waiting. The day of big-budget musical entertainment had begun.

Cameron Mackintosh, the man who would be called the 'Tsar' of such shows, with incredible productions like *Les Misérables* and *Miss Saigon*, was trying to ease a few quid out of me. Cameron was trying to get me to put money in the show. Andrew and Cameron had teamed up with each other and the Royal Shakespeare Company. The RSC's artistic director Trevor Nunn, designer John Napier and choreographer Gillian Lynne were going to put on this extravaganza at the New London Theatre. The theatre had been going for eight years and the only time it had any success was when Bruce Forsyth did a one-man show for a couple of weeks.

There were not many 'angels' clearing their bank accounts to invest. Cameron was so desperate for money that he came and asked me if I would like to invest in the show. Now, I had saved a bit but not so much that I wanted to blow it on a show about cats, in a theatre that nobody liked, on a bunch of songs that didn't sound like hits. I said, 'I don't think so, Cameron.'

It was one of the worst investment decisions that I have ever made in my entire life because that show must have recouped 1,000 per cent and more for the investors. Still, I had no professional regrets. *Cats* put a lot of cream back into my career.

The concept of the show was that all cats are invited to the Jellicle Ball where one cat gets another chance at life. That cat was Grizabella and Judi Dench, who had proved herself musically in *Cabaret* and *The Good Companions*, was to be the one who had lived most of her nine lives. Big Brian

Blessed, who everyone knew from *Z Cars* and *I, Claudius*, was cast as Old Deuteronomy and Wayne Sleep was Mister Mistoffelees. Stephen Tate, who had been Judas, to my Jesus was the aged Gus. Finola Hughes was the White Cat at the beginning of the show.

There was also a girl who used to work with Pan's People in the cast. Her name was Sarah Brightman. I used to give her a lift to Euston Station because she got the train to her home in Hemel Hempstead. Sarah was a good laugh. She had a good sense of humour. She had been in Hot Gossip who were run by Arlene Phillips and had had a hit with a song called 'Starship Trooper'. I'd always thought of Sarah as a dancer and a pop singer. She sang a section at the end of 'Memory', which I was quite taken with, but thought no more of. One day she made me think again. She had recorded a disco version of 'The Sound of Music' and she played it to me. Suddenly, I heard this wonderful soprano voice and it was clear that this voice was more than just a parody of Julie Andrews. I had done to her as a performer what I hate most about this business; I had put her in a pigeon-hole.

We were quite good friends in the show. Sarah told me she had a fascination for piano players. That was her thing. She liked musicians, particularly piano players. She told me about this bloke she was seeing. She wouldn't tell me his name, only that he was a piano player and that she was very taken with him. The piano player turned out to be Andrew Lloyd Webber.

I was asked to play Rum Tum Tugger – who else? He was the pop-star cat, the show's Elvis. I might not have wanted to risk my money but needed a job and it was a great opportunity to work with Trevor Nunn and Gillian Lynne.

I recorded a single, 'Magical Mr. Mistoffelees', as much as a promotion for the show as anything else. It went out in November 1980, and did well on the radio but not in the charts. I sang it on *Michael Parkinson* and other television shows to promote the show for Andrew but it had stiffed as a hit song. Nevertheless, bookings for *Cats* increased.

What concerned me more was me. Could I hack it? I enjoyed dancing but I was not classically trained. Gillian Lynne was a former ballerina and much of the dance in *Cats* would be balletic. I had to start two months before the rest of the cast and get myself to a good enough standard to be accepted as a genuine member of the cast. I worked and worked. I wanted to be in the show, so no matter how much my muscles ached, I kept at it.

When we started the proper rehearsal period, Judi Dench was to play the part of Grizabella. Judi Dench is a fabulous actress and she has gone on to win an Oscar for *Shakespeare in Love* and boss James Bond around in the movies but, like me, she was no ballet dancer. We went to rehearse in Chiswick for six weeks. On the first day, the cast formally met the director Trevor Nunn, Andrew and Gillian. We talked about the general ingredients of the show and how they were going to be achieved. During a tea break Andrew made an announcement: 'I have written a new song for the show which will be sung by Grizabella.' It was all very melodramatic and he added, 'I would like to play it to you.' He put the tape on and the tune of 'Memory' started to play. I had never heard it before. I had heard all the other songs but this was new. I could feel a tingle run down my back and I thought, '*That* is a hit. *That* is the hit song we need for this show to be a hit.'

Andrew had thought 'Magical Mr. Mistoffelees' would 'open' the production but clearly he had decided he needed something stronger. They didn't have a lyric for it. They had half a lyric but they had the tune and some semblance of words but that didn't matter, it had captured me. 'Memory' was not directly from a T. S. Eliot poem. It was bits from Eliot's work and magically woven around an almost new tune of Andrew's. I qualify 'almost' because there are so many tunes playing in his head. It is only when they drop into place – light bulb goes on – that they are polished for their proper setting.

This was to be Dame Judi's song once it was finally written. We were rehearsing every day. We went in each morning and started with an hour's warm up. We had to be able to touch our toes and stretch our hamstrings and tone up our muscles. I was 34 and quite fit but not dancer fit. I couldn't put my legs behind my head or twist my body like a piece of spaghetti.

And I knew that Dame Judi couldn't either. There were a few of us just staying out of the spotlight a little. While Wayne Sleep was leaping all over the place, Dame Judi and I were hiding at the back. Gillian Lynne was a complete maniac about work. She was in her early fifties but she was working like a teenager. Her energy was tremendous! Excitement was building. This was a big chance for Gillian and she was determined not to let it slip by.

Trevor Nunn seemed to be nipping in and out, making points here and there, but when it came to staging the dance, he was clever enough to leave that to Gillian. What Trevor bought to the production was structure and – with John Napier's wonderful set – an environment for the cats to live in. As well as giving every cat a character and a clear sense of who they were.

Dame Judi and I were still at the back during rehearsals, pretending we were kicking our legs up in the air and touching the stars with our toes but we were getting better. We were into it. Then one afternoon Dame Judi was walking across the rehearsal room, just walking, not even dancing. A normal walk, when suddenly, she had a terrible pain in the back of her leg and collapsed on the floor. We all rushed over but there was nothing we could do. She could not walk. She was in agony. Her face was contorted in pain. There was no screaming but I could see how much she was suffering.

Whether the exercise had contributed to it, I don't know, but she'd snapped a hamstring and we were two weeks away from opening.

The first plan was to wait until she'd recovered but that was never going to be possible. The call went out for Elaine Paige. Elaine had gone from the chorus of *Hair* and *Superstar* to play Sandy opposite me in *Grease* and also Rita in the musical *Billy*. *Evita* had made her a name and it was the name that jumped into Andrew's mind after Dame Judi injured herself. It was clear that she couldn't continue with the show.

The one thing that the show needed and it is amazing how these things work out, was someone to sing 'Memory'. Really *sing* it. Dame Judi is a wonderful actress and has had great reviews in musicals and she would have done a great version of that song in her own way. I imagine it would have been performed not unlike Glynis Johns's 'Send in the Clowns'. It would have been an actor's performance but without a big theatrical finish. What it needed was a big voice. Elaine Paige had one. With Elaine performing the showcase number, *Cats* had its big finale. Someone who could really belt out the song. Streisand had a hit with 'Memory'. Elaine recorded it – 158 people have – and performed it on many television programmes to promote the show. It was not until the evening of the first preview that Cameron had gathered together the last £10,000 of the budget and even then Andrew had personally guaranteed a giant chunk of the money.

Opening night at the rubbish dump arrived. I was still wondering how the audience was going to receive *Cats*. The feline creatures were everywhere, leaping out of dustbins, scooting and crawling around John Napier's set, which was built to cat's scale, about three and half times normal size. I knew audiences would be intrigued by the set. The best seats were reserved for those seated on the revolving stage and as the overture began, the stage slowly began to revolve. The audience found themselves moving. Cats eyes flashed from every corner of the theatre. The audience was completely disorientated. What a great opening. No one cared about the plot. This was all production.

Which is where the magic of Trevor and Andrew and Cameron came in. The concept, the perception, the vision. That is what tilted *Cats* into being such an enormous hit. It was as if Gillian Lynne had squeezed every ounce of energy into every dancer's leotard. And now it was bursting on to the stage of the New London Theatre.

Midnight, not a sound from the pavement,
Has the moon lost her memory?
She is smiling alone.
In the lamplight the withered leaves collect at my feet
And the wind begins to moan.
Memory – all alone in the moonlight
I can smile at the old days
I was beautiful then.

When Elaine sang 'Memory' for the first time live in public it tore the place apart. This was Grizabella the Glamour Cat at full throttle. It was sheer musical theatre and what you always want – a showstopper!

As Rum Tum Tugger I was like the Esso advert – a tiger in the tank. I could not be tied down. Someone called him a 'pop-star puss' and he was. He was a strutting Gary Glitter, a capricious cat who seemed to jump here, there and everywhere. My opening number had a big dance break in the middle and I thought, 'There's no way I can stay on stage and cut this, dancing with all these fantastic cats. I have to think of something else.'

My plot was to spray the audience with perfume, a play on

'smelly cats'. I put this to Trevor Nunn but he thought Health and Safety might not take too kindly to me spraying the audience as if they smelt bad. We agreed I could run around the audience and fool around, sit on people's laps, stroke their hair, and behave like a cat. A very cool cat, of course.

When Prince Charles came to see the show I found the famous bald spot and ruffled the hair around it. When Princess Grace of Monaco came, I sat on her lap. This way I was able to get through Rum Tum Tugger without having to dance. I did it with comedy and that remained the style for Rum Tum Tugger thereafter.

Even a bomb scare didn't take the sparkle off the opening night. The audience loved us but we could not take our bows. Brian Blessed had to go on stage, and ask people to leave the theatre telling them, 'This is serious.' A man with an Irish accent had called saying there were three bombs in the stage revolve. Nothing was ever found. As it turned out, it was a new form of musical theatre that had exploded.

10
Very Good Friends

'No Quasimodo jokes,' says Penny as she and Vince drive around Paris. 'People always make Quasimodo jokes at Notre Dame.'

'Yeah,' says Vince. 'It's enough to give anyone the hump.'

– *Just Good Friends*, November 1986

T im Rice had a bee in his bonnet about Richard the Lionheart and the Crusades. He and Andrew Lloyd Webber had developed a children's musical around that theme called *Come Back, Richard, Your Country Needs You*. Years later Andrew was working on his own material and Tim created *Blondel*, a two-act play with music by Stephen Oliver who had won attention for scoring the Royal Shakespeare Company's *Nicholas Nickleby*.

It was about King Richard being rescued from a Continental prison by the minstrel Blondel. Cameron asked me to play Blondel. I had a backing group called the Blondettes, which tells you something about the show. The show portrayed Blondel as a minstrel pop singer. One of the newspapers called it a 'polished pantomime', which was close. Despite some other, more disparaging notices, we moved after 87 performances from the Old Vic to the Aldwych Theatre in the West End where we played 278 performances. That long run was really down to the backing of Tim and Cameron Mackintosh, for *Blondel* was simply something Tim had to see through to free himself. Cameron had the big hit with *Cats* and wanted to do this musical with Tim Rice directed by Peter James but it was a classic case of something not being quite right and no one knowing.

I didn't know that the best job of my career to date was just around the corner. Soon everyone would hear about *Just Good Friends*. John Sullivan had seen me in the television play *A Little Roccoco*. I came home one evening and there was a script for a new TV sitcom waiting for me.

I read it. It was the first episode of *Just Good Friends* – the pilot – and I thought, 'This is terrific.' I thought it was funny and that it was perfect for me. I didn't quite understand why they wanted to see me because I was in musical theatre and had done very little television work. It was arranged that I go to the BBC to meet with the producer, Ray Butt, and John Sullivan, the writer. We were there to talk about a pilot show.

I turned up at the BBC Centre and sitting in the reception was this very attractive girl called Jan Francis, who I vaguely recognized from seeing on TV. We introduced ourselves to each other. I said that I thought the script was good and she agreed. We were trying to laugh off our nerves, rather than be dreadfully serious about the audition. We made each other laugh and seemed to get on quite well. Which is always good if you are going to be reading with someone.

But at that point we didn't know that we were going to be reading. We hoped that perhaps we might get away with just seeing them. We went in to meet Ray Butt, who is a short man and looks like Kenneth Connor from the *Carry On* films. He was very South London. He kept calling us *mes enfants* which always made me die. John Sullivan was very quiet and intro-verted like a lot of writers and also from South London.

We told them we liked the script and then they asked us to read. I was this working-class character from Walthamstow and Jan played this slightly aristocratic, middle-class girl from Chipping Ongar, Essex. John got the idea from reading the problem pages in one of his wife's magazines. There was a letter from a woman who, five years after being left at the altar, had once again met the man who jilted her. The woman's problem was that to her surprise – not to say distress – she found there was still something about him that she liked.

Enter Vince's and Penny's rekindled romance into my life and the public's imagination. What was so clever was that here was a situation comedy that had an ongoing storyline with a constant cliffhanger. Would Vince have the bottle to accompany Penny to the altar a second time around? I thought the writing was excellent. Jan and I read and the others seemed quite happy. I thought it was a wonderful opportunity. John and Ray seemed to know what they wanted. I later got a call saying that the part was mine.

Jan was not sure if she wanted to play Penny. She had a background in straight drama, including *Secret Army*. She had not done much work in front of a live audience since the early part of her career. And working with a live sitcom audience was like doing a first night every week. It was always going to be nerve-racking, no matter how many times you did it. You can work in front of a live audience. You can work in front of a camera. Put the two together and it becomes more difficult. The trick is to work the camera and not the audience in the studio. They are there simply to supply the laughs. The real audience is sitting at home watching the television. It was something we both had to learn and as the show progressed the critics – as well as the public – agreed we had. Because Jan and I got on so well as people, I think we were able to communicate this through our characters. But there was a nervous waiting period before we became a television couple.

Jan wanted to see three episodes to help her make a decision! It made absolute sense to read three episodes to see if the quality of writing was sustained. In the meantime, John and Ray came to see me in *Cats*. I took them for a drink after the show and they told me they were still awaiting Jan's decision. They were very keen for her to do it. Being a compulsive worrier, I thought they might not go ahead without her. I had no clue we were going to make a little bit of television history, although I did believe that we were on to a winning series. So I was crossing everything.

Another two scripts arrived. They were equally funny. Jan decided that she would do the show. I was very relieved. At that point, we were booked only to do the pilot show, which meant that if one of us didn't cut the mustard, they could recast.

We did some filming for the episode. Then, we did the first show in front of a live audience. We were both very nervous. It was a new experience for us but we enjoyed it. It went very well. Jan and I were getting on like a house on fire and the studio audience really took to the show, which was very encouraging. John and Ray seemed exceptionally pleased. We all felt that we were on to a winner and that the BBC would commission a series with Jan and me playing Penny and Vince. Ray Butt worked fast and did not bugger about. He was a really good workman-like producer who knew what he wanted and I thought he was a terrific influence on John. He and John were like a couple of brothers, Ray being the elder. John would say, 'We've been around since dinosaurs ruled the world.'

John had started off as a scene shifter at the BBC because he didn't know quite how to get into television even though he had been writing. He had already done *Citizen Smith* with Robert Lindsay and *Only Fools and Horses* with David Jason.

This was John's third attempt after two hits under the auspices of Ray Butt, who would quite happily edit John's work. There was nothing luvvie about their relationship or indeed about the show. There was no theatricality about it. Ray was very experienced and knew where the laughs were. He was a great teacher for me.

I had done a sitcom in 1979, *Two Up, Two Down*, with Su Pollard. We were two revolutionary squatters who took over a terraced house in Manchester, much to the annoyance of the newlyweds who had just moved in. It was not the greatest sitcom but was very useful and meant I was not a novice at the format.

One thing I did learn about sitcoms, *the* most important thing, is to learn your lines. You get the script on Monday and the following Sunday you have two hours to record the show. There's very little time. You have to know your lines well enough so that you can say them automatically without thinking, because if you don't, when the red light goes on and the studio audience starts laughing, it's quite easy for your memory to go for a walk in the park. I know that sounds like a very obvious thing, but there is knowing your lines and *really* knowing your lines. Some episodes were just the two of us and that meant 60 pages of dialogue to be learned in five days. You might have 10 pages a week on a movie.

Many sitcoms seem a little hysterical. This is usually because a lot of the time the actors are nervous and groping for their lines. Plus they're delivering laugh lines for the first time and are never really sure what the audience's reaction will be.

We did the pilot and it went tremendously well. Vince – like John Sullivan – was always trying to give up smoking and he had this placebo, a plastic cigarette. In the first show Vince tells Penny about a visit to an acupuncturist to try and help him give up smoking. Penny asks Vince, 'Did you feel a prick?' Vince replies, 'Well, I did feel a bit silly.' There was something so special about the writing. This was a sex and class war but there was never anything too unkind. I was really pleased with it.

John Howard Davies, the BBC Head of Comedy at that time, was not convinced that I was right for the part of Vince.

John had been an actor and had played Oliver Twist in the classic 1948 film. He had seen the pilot video and wasn't sure about me. He felt that I tended to underplay Vince. I felt that the writing and the reality of the situation was such, that this was not a sitcom to be played in the style of *Hi De Hi* or *'Allo, 'Allo*. It was about real people, in real situations, that the audience at home could identify with. It was not a farce. I think John Howard Davies would have preferred – and to be fair he only had one episode on which to judge – that my performance was a little more 'Jack the Lad'. I thought that the essence of Vince's character was that he wasn't flash; he was naïve. You didn't need to overplay him. The lines were so well written that it was unnecessary to hit the back wall and that was one of the compliments that John Sullivan paid me. What he liked was that I was letting the lines play themselves.

Ray Butt decided to do some intensive research. He screened the pilot for some BBC secretaries who endorsed, as an unbiased audience, his support for me. I am grateful that John Howard Davies was big enough to change his mind and allowed me to do the show. We went on to make three more series and a couple of specials. A Christmas show brought in 22 million viewers and is in the Top Ten of the most-watched shows of all time. *Just Good Friends* had a regular audience of close to 15 million and won a BAFTA award. I was also nominated for 'Best Comedy Performance'. *Just Good Friends* changed my life. It reflected the power of television, especially in the mid-1980s. People didn't have satellite or cable television, so when a show took off, the whole nation watched.

I was on tour with *Blondel* in Bath prior to it reopening at the Old Vic when the first episode was shown. I didn't watch it because I was on stage but the next morning I was in Bath city centre and people kept coming up to me and saying, 'Saw the show last night – great.' That was when I knew it was a hit. The great thing about the public is you can tell if something works. You don't have to wait for the ratings because you can tell from people's reactions. There is a distinctive difference between people being genuine about how they feel about something and people just saying what they think you want to hear. People were very excited about that show. The only thing I was concerned about was whether we could sustain their excitement over the coming weeks. We could and became a very, very big hit. My instinct, my nose, in reading it for the first time was correct. It went to Number 3 in the ratings the following week.

It gave me a lot of clout. Vince was a lovable rogue and audiences, both men and women, identified with him. He was the lower-working-class guy and she was a middle-class girl. There was a lot of newspaper and magazine interest in me and I had lots of requests for interviews. Journalists would try and equate me with the character of Vince.

You wait all your life as a performer to get your name known. What's important is that you make sure that your character isn't more identifiable than you. On soaps like *Coronation Street* and *EastEnders* the character name is usually better known than the performer. I was more interested in using Vince Pinner to promote Paul Nicholas.

I wanted to exploit my own name and show how different I was from Vince Pinner: So instead of having the newspapers try to portray me as Vince Pinner, I made sure I had lots of photographs taken with Linzi and the kids to give myself an image that was the complete antithesis of Vince.

The whole fame thing was very interesting. I didn't particularly like it. I'm not someone who enjoys too much attention. People are very nice; they only want your autograph, but it made me a little bit uncomfortable. I was a little embarrassed by it. I was voted the Sexiest Man on Television and had all the attention anyone could want. I was also elected Britain's

Best Dressed Man. I think that was because Vince wore rather nifty suits. My family went into shock. I've always been a bit of a scruff.

I was enjoying my success. The family was settled and we were happier than we'd been for a long time. I had been with Linzi for fifteen years and we thought it was time that we got married. I've never liked to rush into things and she was beginning to think that we were never going to get married. And then, suddenly, I wanted to. It did seem about time I married the woman I had loved for so long. It felt right for both of us and for the children. We got married at Haringey Town Hall, not the most romantic spot in the world. I was a little bit late. Deliberately. I drove around the block just to make them nervous. Linzi saw the funny side of it.

Linzi became pregnant not long after we were married and we were delighted. Sadly, at four months, she lost the baby. We were in our late thirties and felt that our chance of having another baby had gone. We were both nervous about trying for another child but, after a lot of soul searching, we changed our minds. We thought it would be nice for Alexander to have a little brother or sister and great for us to have another baby in the house.

Carmen was born in May 1986. We now had four children but that was the first birth I had attended. We went to hospital at around midnight and we waited for seven hours and she was born at seven o'clock in the morning. It had been an anxious time for us. When you have lost a baby you are never quite certain what will happen next time. We felt blessed and very lucky.

Once I had that break with *Just Good Friends* my aim was to ensure my family's security. When you are in a profession that is extremely fickle and you have responsibilities to your family, you have to provide as well as you can and when you can. I was now fortunate to be able to do that. *Just Good*

Friends had helped to make my name and that was good for all of us.

The great thing about showbusiness is that you're never sure what your next job is going to be, or who you will be working with. Before the first series of *Just Good Friends*, I got a call from my agent telling me that he'd had an enquiry for me on a film called *Invitation to the Wedding*. I asked who was in it. He said, 'Two knights.' I said, 'Two nights? That's not very long, I was hoping for at least six weeks.' He said, 'No, *the* two knights – Sir John Gielgud and Sir Ralph Richardson!'

I have said that showbusiness is fickle, but it is also packed by strange coincidences and paths that cross and criss-cross. My friend Paul Jabara – Herod to my Jesus – and I had written a song in 1974 titled 'When You're a Lord'. It was for a movie called *The Lords of Flatbush* about a Brooklyn street gang. Sylvester Stallone, Perry King and Henry Winkler – still to become the Fonz in *Happy Days* – starred as New York gang members.

The producer of the movie was Joseph Brooks. He had made a fortune writing songs like 'I'd Like to Teach the World to Sing' – the Coca-Cola anthem – and the world-wide hit 'You Light up My Life' for Debbie Boone, Pat Boone's daughter. He had a lot of money – and he wanted to spend it on his wife Susan Brooks, who was an actress.

He was very much in love with his wife and wanted to do something special for her. The best thing you can do for any actress is put her in a starring role in a movie. *Invitation to the Wedding* was to be filmed in Britain and he wanted nothing but the best talent to co-star with his wife.

Not only did he get Sir John Gielgud, he also got Sir Ralph Richardson as well as the lighting genius of Freddie Young – *Lawrence of Arabia* no less. Terrific actors like John Standing,

Elizabeth Shepherd and Ronald Lacey were also cast. And me. And I had the most difficult job.

Joseph Brooks produced and directed the film and composed the music. Unfortunately, Joe suffered from a terrible stammer and when he became stressed, it would get considerably worse. The part Joe wanted to see me for was an American on a visit to the Home Counties, who meets and falls in love with a young girl, played by his wife. I was on holiday in Cornwall when I got the call and they brought me back to London to do a screen test. Joseph Brooks was besotted with his wife and, as a result, was very particular about who he cast as the leading man.

I did the film test and got the part. A week later, I started on the film, which had been written by William Fairchild. It was the story of a girl who was supposed to marry one man but falls in love with another (my character) and ends up leaving her intended at the altar in order to be with me. It was a little like Dustin Hoffman and Katharine Ross in *The Graduate*. It was all set in and around a typical English village. Sir Ralph Richardson played the local vicar and Sir John Gielgud was an American evangelist.

I had to learn to ride because there were a couple of romantic scenes with Susan and myself on horseback. Learning to ride was the easy part. It was doing the love scenes when things became really difficult.

Joe Brooks was very possessive of his young wife. He had the potential to be very jealous. Susan was very beautiful and I suspected that Joe thought that every man on the set, including myself, was after her. Joe would get particularly tense whenever we had to play any romantic moments and I sensed that we might have some problems when it came to our first screen kiss.

The day of our big love scene arrived and poor Joe was getting extremely agitated. He'd worked it all out. He took me to one side and said, 'Remember, Paul, this is not *Emmanuel*. This is a light romantic comedy and the scene should be played as such, OK?' I said, 'Absolutely, Joe.' 'OK, Paul, I want you to take Susan in your arms and hold her – not too tight. I want you to look into her eyes, tell her that you love her and very slowly, very gently kiss her. I will count to three and you will break. Got it?' he asked. 'Got it, Joe.' I'm thinking, 'This guy's lost it.' So the camera was set up and Freddie Young lit the scene beautifully. Susan and I rehearsed the scene but without the kiss. Joe by now was getting a little edgy but was doing his best to control his stammer that was becoming a little more pronounced by the minute. 'OK g-g-guys,' he said. 'Are w-w-we set? Speed, c-c-camera.' He whispered the word 'Action.' Susan and I were standing facing each other. I took her into my arms. Not too tight. We looked into each other's eyes. I told her that I loved her. Then slowly, ever so slowly, our heads moved together for the 'gentle' kiss. Everything was going according to plan but in that millisecond before our lips touched, I thought, 'Sod it!' and I gave her the biggest tongue sandwich I could muster. Joe is in shock. He can barely speak. His stammer is completely out of control. 'O-o-o-o-o-o-one, t-t-t-t-t-t-two.' He couldn't get the numbers out. Finally, blue in the face, he screams, 'C-c-c-c-c-c-c-cut!!!' I looked at Susan, Susan looked at me and we both collapsed in a heap, screaming with laughter.

For me the bonus was working with Sir John Gielgud and Sir Ralph Richardson. Sir Ralph was quite elderly and finding it difficult to remember his words. He needed help. I always felt sorry for him because here was this great actor who was now having to rely to some extent on cue cards because his memory was beginning to fail quite badly.

The wonderful thing about Sir Ralph was that when he did deliver his lines the marvellous twinkle and great charm was still there. No matter how difficult he found it, the years could not diminish his skill as an actor. He was always superb.

Sir John Gielgud was famous for having a very distinctive voice. He was also famous for not being terribly good with accents. In the film, he was playing an American evangelist who flies in from the southern state of Alabama, to officiate at the wedding. I was full of great anticipation. This was to be a moment I would never forget. I was about to play my first scene with one of the world's greatest actors.

So the scene was set with us all seated at the dinner table waiting for him to appear. On 'action', Sir John was supposed to burst into the room and announce his arrival. 'Speed, camera, action!' The door flies open and in walks Sir John Gielgud as the American evangelist, dressed all in white. White cowboy boots, white suit and a large white stetson. He opens his mouth and delivers his opening line.

'Howdy, folks. I've just flown in from Alabama and I'm right pleased to be here and happy to meet ya all.'

There was a stunned silence. It was the worst American accent any of us had ever heard. It sounded like he had just flown in from Reykjavik not Alabama. Added to this was that he looked completely ridiculous in his white cowboy outfit. Up until that point I had been feeling very reverential about the whole enterprise but as soon as he opened his mouth, I got the giggles. I did my best but I could not contain myself. What began as a stifled giggle grew into hysterical laughter and, to make matters worse, the rest of the cast were acting as if they hadn't noticed and that this was Sir John at his most brilliant. Which made me laugh even more. Finally, Sir John walked over and very nicely clipped me around the ear and said, 'Stop laughing, dear boy.' It was difficult but, like Sir Ralph Richardson, he was a very charming man and I could see that he knew why I was laughing.

When the film came out *Just Good Friends* had hit the

screen and was very popular, so they switched the advertising in favour of me. I am sorry to say the movie never made any great impact. The thrill for me was working with these two icons of British theatre. Something I will always cherish.

I was about to be made bankrupt. On television. My attempts to avoid being solely identified as Vince Pinner had succeeded. I was now Neil Walsh, an altogether different character. But, thankfully, one that the British viewers liked almost as much as Vince. From the start Neil had the whiff of a man who does dodgy deals with even dodgier people. The audience first saw him in the bankruptcy court over a less than solid cement deal owing the bank £129,000. The chap in front of him was declared bankrupt for £2 million and Neil shook his head and said, 'That's where I went wrong. Not enough ambition.'

They called the series *Bust* and it did very well for ITV, pulling in more than 11 million viewers on a Friday night. Phyllis Logan co-starred in the first series as my beleaguered wife Sheila. Belinda Lang took over the part for the second series. Geraldine Alexander was Janet the bank trustee handling my financial affairs. It was the mid-1980s. The time of Thatcher, yuppies and mobile phones and it was perfect.

I felt a change of gear from *Just Good Friends* was right for me, as the public were so used to me doing comedy and this was drama. It would give me the chance to show I could play something else. Cab drivers liked the show, so it was obviously working. We did two series of *Bust* until Neil got out of bankruptcy.

I seemed to have found the Midas touch for television. I was in great demand for all sorts of work. Celeste Holm, who in 1956 had co-starred with Frank Sinatra, Grace Kelly and Bing Crosby in *High Society*, agreed to appear with me at a Royal Command Performance for the Queen. We did 'Who Wants to Be a Millionaire?' from *High Society* and it was very well received.

It seemed I was flavour of the year. When everyone – agents, advisers, Linzi and myself – thought I could do no wrong on television, I made a terrible mistake. I started working with animals.

The series was again for ITV. It was titled *Close to Home* and was about a divorced vet bringing up two children and fending off the incursions of his former wife. It was based on an American sitcom called *Starting from Scratch* which Greg Dyke – now Director General of the BBC and then Programming Director for LWT – had picked up. The writer-creator of the US version was Brian Cooke, who had written shows like *Man About the House* and *Father, Dear Father* in Britain. He had moved to California and got *Starting from Scratch* on the air. He was going to redo the scripts for British TV, along with other writers. The plan was to adopt the American method of 'team' writing. Sadly, Brian Cooke was not around to oversee the team's efforts. We had a good cast. Angharad Rees, Demelza in *Poldark*, was my former wife and the kids were played by Lucy Benjamin and Andrew Reag.

It was quite a nice series but it didn't work terribly well. My veterinarian James Shepherd was never going to worry James Herriot and *All Creatures Great and Small*. There were lots of jokes about tarnished goldfish and parrot gags, some sexual innuendo on the mating habits of cats. That sort of thing.

They thought the idea of me and little animals would work. I was looking for a new series and I wanted to work for London Weekend again, having had quite a good track record with them: one hit series. I listened to the wrong people because when I looked at a video of the American version I thought it was OK. It worked in America but was not *that* good. By the time it had been rewritten for an English cast, it was even less funny. It just didn't work.

Simply, the scripts were not funny or sophisticated enough.

It was not enough to have furry animals and a bloke who smiles a lot. We did two series and I admire LWT for trying. They did their best but despite their efforts, it just didn't work. It was a big mistake. I should have trusted my instinct and that was a turning point for me.

No one wants to be involved in something that is a miss, particularly when it is as high profile as a prime television series. The terrible thing for an artist on television is if you find yourself in a non-runner you are the one who suffers. The writers may go on to write something else, the producer could go on and make another programme but you, the star, are labelled as the failure for the show and have to bear the cross. It does you no favours at all and it is very difficult to recover from it. The trade-off is absolutely right. If you are a success you receive the plaudits that go with that.

Since that moment with *Close to Home* I decided that whatever I do, I would listen to people but if I had any doubts about something or did not believe in something 100 per cent myself, I wouldn't be swayed. I have been in showbusiness all of my life and I am going to get it wrong sometimes. I am going to miss certain things but most of the time I get it right because of experience. It is what I do for a living.

I was angry with myself for getting involved in *Close to Home*. I chose to do it. I thought TV was good for me and that rather blunted my decision-making process. It comes down to what is on the page and what the lines and stories are. Nothing else matters. I resolved never to lose sight of that again. And to stay in control of my material as much as possible. Even if it meant walking the tightrope.

11
The Musical Man

There's one born every minute.

– Phineas T. Barnum, 1861

T elevision is like a drug – especially when you are on it. It had given me an overwhelming share of fame but it had also taught me a severe lesson about choices. And control. *Just Good Friends* had been very good to me but I had to maintain control and not end up like Frankenstein and the Monster. With *Close to Home* I had allowed myself to be caught up in a Rolf Harris world of vets and pets without, sadly, the success that Rolf has achieved talking to the animals.

I knew I had to keep my eye on the ball. Which is why I had worked so hard to separate myself from Vince. I had the pop world, some movies and the theatre but it was Vince who brought me to the public's attention. He was funny and charming and with a lot of heart. He was also a little bit of a rogue. Britain is one nation that loves the 'cheeky-chappie' image whether he is a Max Miller or a little more dodgy, like George Cole in *Minder*. Vince was a man-about-Basildon version of both. He made me very well known.

Some actors I have worked with can stand at stage doors talking about themselves for hours, to people that they don't know, and they are very comfortable with that. They make all kinds of public appearances such as opening fêtes. The only thing I ever opened was the Truck Fest in Peterborough. It is a festival to celebrate big trucks. I was driven to a hotel and I took Linzi with me to hold one hand and Alexander to hold the other. I was flown from the hotel by helicopter to a speedway arena. It was so embarrassing. We landed right in the middle of the arena and our arrival was announced over the loudspeaker to somewhat indifferent applause. People were waiting to see the 'star' arrive and I was put into this open-top car and driven round the speedway arena, waving to people like a monkey. This chap asked me, 'Shall we go around again?' I said, 'No. I think once is enough.' I spent all day sitting at a table signing autographs. The most common comment I heard was, 'Oh, you look much younger on the television.' Thanks!

I wasn't very good at being a TV personality. I wasn't comfortable dealing with that sort of thing. It is necessary. You have to be polite to the general public and you sign autographs and you say 'how lovely' and people are generally very nice. I find people don't hassle you, but to be presented as 'Paul Nicholas' outside of a performing context I have always found very, very difficult. With a couple of exceptions – despite the very good money – I have never done it. What, ironically, television did do for me was lead me back into the theatre. Theatregoers are fascinated by a television 'name' and that attraction makes them turn out to see you in shows. This was another reason I had to keep Vince Pinner and Paul Nicholas so separate. Audiences were not going to see Vince Pinner in *The Pirates of Penzance*. They were going to see Paul Nicholas.

We played *Pirates* at the Manchester Opera House in 1984. It was a huge success and Michael Ball's first job. It was interesting to watch him as Frederick for he had a wonderful voice and was clearly a star-in-waiting. He was also cruel to me – in a kind way.

The show does not begin until the Pirate King gets on board and stands on the prow of the boat. The overture starts and the boat moves on to the stage and the show begins. I don't like to arrive on stage for the night's performance too early. I don't want to go off the boil. Most of the cast appeared promptly at the five-minute call, which meant that they were usually standing around waiting for me to appear. I used to arrive on stage about thirty seconds before 'curtain up'. The cast was aware of this and decided, led by Michael Ball, to exact their revenge. One night, without me knowing, they pre-recorded the overture on tape. I was in my dressing room preparing for the show that night. It didn't occur to me that there had been no 'five-minute' call. I was just finishing my second cup of tea with my feet up on the dressing-room table, about to light another cigarette, when suddenly, over the tannoy, I heard the overture begin to play. Panic set in and my dresser and I started to throw on my costume, mike pack and make-up simultaneously. I headed for the dressing-room door, pulling my thigh-length leather boots on as I went. I flung open the door and, to my surprise, the entire cast was standing there, pointing at me and roaring with laughter. I was never late again.

Harold Fielding, whom Robert Stigwood had outmanoeuvred over *Superstar*, remained a powerful theatrical figure. He was a great showman and a very experienced producer. And a fan of legends. He had staged one at the London Palladium in 1983: *Singin' in the Rain*. It cashed in on much of the MGM film's screenplay and used seven of the songs including, of course, the title song. Tommy Steele had adapted the movie and he directed and co-starred with the late Roy Castle. It was a magnificent production and theatrical achievement.

I got a chance to do something from the past too. While I had been charging around Britain trying to be a rock star in 1965 the show *Charlie Girl* had been staged by Harold Fielding with Joe Brown and Dame Anna Neagle and a young

Derek Nimmo, who was establishing himself on television with series like *All Gas and Gaiters* and *The World of Wooster*. The updated Cinderella story had started life as a summer show. It went on to break house records at the Adelphi Theatre in the West End. The show had a colourful beginning – hated by the critics but loved by audiences – with Anna Neagle acknowledging the happy ending with: 'It's marvellous. Flippin' well marvellous.'

The show's music was written by David Heneker, who in 1958 had created *Expresso Bongo*, which was based on the career of Tommy Steele. He later wrote *Half a Sixpence* in which Tommy starred both in London and on Broadway. The show was produced by Harold Fielding.

In the mid-1960s, Gerry Marsden of the Pacemakers was very hot and took over the leading role of 'Joe' from Joe Brown. Two decades later, I was cast in the part. My co-stars were Cyd Charisse, Dora Bryan, Nicholas Parsons and Mark Wynter. I had watched Cyd as a small boy in those MGM musicals, partnering legends like Gene Kelly in *Singin' in the Rain* and Fred Astaire in the movie *Silk Stockings*. It was a dream come true. I danced with the woman who had danced with Gene Kelly and Fred Astaire and that's one of the things that makes showbusiness exciting. It's unpredictable. Cyd was every inch a lady, every inch a star.

It was 1986 and I was at the height of my popularity and made my first appearance at the most famous theatre in the world: the London Palladium. I was appearing in a record-breaking season of *Cinderella* with Des O'Connor and Dame Anna Neagle. Des is someone I admire. He is the true professional and has been in the business even longer than I have. He is a perfect example of an artist with staying power. He's had to take a lot of ribbing over the years but is still a star and now has the number one chat show on television.

Dame Anna was 80 plus when I worked with her and,

again, a true pro. She was playing the fairy godmother and I think she had a soft spot for me. She was forever telling me, 'If only I were fifty years younger . . .' I was extremely flattered.

With my career going so well, I was looking for an agent. I needed a good one. I found two: Billy Marsh and Jan Kennedy. Billy was a very experienced agent. He went a long way back and was very well respected in the business. He handled such great acts as Bruce Forsyth, Norman Wisdom and Morecambe and Wise.

Billy was a small, softly spoken man who loved to smoke one cigarette after the other. One of the fascinating things about watching him smoke was that he did it in such a way that at least one and a half inches of ash would hang precariously at the end of his fag. It was very stressful wondering whether Billy would manage to get the cigarette from his mouth to the ashtray without the ash spilling all over his suit. Most of the time he didn't make it. Indeed Eric Morecambe used to quip that when he died he was leaving Billy 10 per cent of his ashes, to be thrown over his lapels.

Jan Kennedy was a former artist who had become an agent and Billy was her mentor. You're never quite sure what you're going to get when you change agents. They all make you feel as if you are the most important client in the world, until you join them. Thereafter you become one of forty other artists who proceed to drive them nuts. All you can ever hope for with an agent is that they graft. Jan Kennedy is certainly a grafter. She told me she could get me great deals doing touring productions of major musicals. She also told me I was a star and I half believed her. It was the beginning of a long and happy association and I owe a lot to her and Billy.

Jan was as good as her word and I was cast to play Phineas T. Barnum in the first national tour of *Barnum*. She phoned me one day and said, 'Can you walk a tightrope?' I said, 'How much?' *Barnum* is probably the most demanding musical any performer could undertake. He was the ultimate showman. Michael Crawford had starred as Barnum at the Palladium for a 20-month run in Cy Coleman's and Mark Bramble's circus musical.

Barnum is considered to be extremely demanding for the actor playing the lead role. Other than the usual acting, singing and dancing, there are certain other skills that are necessary in order to play the part: juggling, unicycling, trampolining and, most difficult of all, learning to walk a tightrope from one side of the stage to the other, singing at the same time. Jim Dale, who was the original *Barnum* on Broadway, during rehearsals said, 'I can actually walk a wire.' That feat was not in the show until Jim Dale performed it. Thereafter every Barnum who followed him had to walk the wire.

This extra dimension led to a certain mystique surrounding *Barnum*. I was in my mid-forties and because of this some people felt it might prove too taxing for me. I wasn't 100 per cent sure myself. I started training. I was sent to Circus Circus, a casino in Las Vegas where the punters gamble surrounded by circus performers doing their acts.

The last time I had been in Las Vegas was in the mid-1970s where at the Hilton International I had seen the King himself, Elvis, perform. Elvis had always been one of my heroes and at that time he still had it. It was an afternoon show in one of those typical Las Vegas lounge environments. Elvis was in great voice. Looked fantastic but seemed a little bored with it all and at one point threw a glass of water into his guitarist's face. Elvis thought it was funny. There was a token eight or nine middle-aged women standing at the foot of the stage. Elvis placed white scarves around their necks. It somehow didn't seem worthy of the King. He was the original, both in his appearance and in his music. It's such a shame that he went into the army, had his hair cut, did those lousy movies and met that dreadful tailor!

I was met at the airport by my trainers for *Barnum*, Terry and Danuta Parsons. Terry was a former clown and was in charge of all the safety aspects connected with the circus skills in the show. Danuta was a trapeze artist who was appearing at Circus Circus and had a wide range of circus skills. They were good teachers.

I began learning on a wire that was only a foot off the ground. After about three days, I progressed to a three-foot wire and finally a wire that was ten feet off the ground. It was a long and at times frustrating process but, after six weeks, I was good enough to begin the rehearsals proper with the rest of the cast. All the preparation and learning to walk the wire were now to be put to the test. The wire-walking occurs at the end of Act I. Barnum is going through a personal dilemma of whether to leave his wife Charity for Jenny Lind, the 'Swedish Nightingale', whom he had brought over from Sweden to appear in one of his shows. The tight-rope walk is there to show the emotional tight-rope that Barnum is walking. Jenny Lind stands on a platform on one side of the proscenium arch and Barnum is on the other. The cast fixes a wire between the two. In most venues that meant that the wire was approximately forty feet long. Jenny proffers her hand and Barnum begins to walk. That was the most difficult moment. Michael being Michael used to go for a record every time – trying to get across as many times as he could without falling off.

I never worried about that because first of all I knew that audiences like you to fall off; it sustains their interest a bit longer. I didn't want to put myself under that kind of pressure and if I fell I would look across to Jenny and say, 'You'd better be worth it.' The only time I felt under pressure was on a press night, because I didn't want to give the newspapers ammunition to be negative about the show.

I used to fall off quite a lot. My record was six times in one night. After the sixth time the audience thought they were going to miss the last bus home. You had to complete it because musically it led into the end of the first act. The worst thing about falling off was ripping my trousers and exposing my bottom and having to complete the walk with my arse hanging out. The audience loved it and found it very amusing.

I had a difficult trampoline jump at the beginning of the show that resulted in the only accident I had as Barnum. It involved me jumping from a trampoline to where my wife Charity is seated in a box, looking down on the stage. Having landed on the small platform next to the box, I was to swing round and give her a kiss. This manoeuvre required that after making the jump I grabbed the bar that was protruding from the little platform which then secured my landing. I ran, jumped on the trampoline and reached for the bar. It wasn't there. I missed. There was this marvellous *Road Runner* moment where I hung for a split second in mid-air before crashing on to the trampoline below. For a moment I thought I had broken my back but I was just winded. I felt so embarrassed missing the jump. I immediately went back and redid it to great applause from the audience.

The other complicated moments involved the death slide. At the end of the show Barnum runs to the very top of the auditorium and slides down a rope over the audience's head, on to the stage. This device is not unlike that which the army uses to transport soldiers across rivers. It looked very spectacular but it wasn't that dangerous. The hard part was climbing the stairs to the top of the auditorium and changing costume before sliding down the rope. All to be done in three minutes.

Barnum was a good show. The only disappointment with *Barnum* was that I always felt sorry for the children who came to see it. The advertising suggested that this was a real circus show, complete with animals. There were none. Although there were a number of circus skills involved, the show was quite dark at times.

It was a great exercise for me. The physical demands of eight shows a week kept me in shape. They say you can't teach an old dog new tricks but I'm a living example that you can.

Barnum started off as a man who ran a freak show. He was a purveyor of bearded ladies and all sorts of so-called curiosities. He introduced the first African elephant to America and called it Jumbo. When the elephant died, he had it stuffed and continued to exhibit it. How sensible. He built the American Museum which he packed with weird attractions. His sole motivation was to get the punters in and make money. He was a wonderful showman.

Harold Fielding was also a wonderful showman. Harold knew how to bring people into the theatre. He was the original producer of *Barnum*. I'd watched Harold and people like him over the years and detail mattered to them. Harold was very keen to make sure the box-office staff were on the case. Without a good box-office, you don't sell tickets. He was excellent at making sure that all the coach firms and party-bookers were given good deals and taken care of. He knew the importance of good advertising and was one of the few producers who didn't take investors. He always used his own money.

I became a little bit imbued with the spirit of Barnum. It began to make me think about what I was doing with my life. How artists – including myself – were slaves to the phone call. I wanted more control. At the end of the 1980s I began to think about getting involved in production. I am a performer first and foremost. I'm not prepared to give up that life and become a businessman. I saw myself as a performer who produces, rather than a producer who performs.

I did *Barnum* for a long time and it was very successful. We came to the West End with it and did a fantastic sell-out Christmas season at the Dominion in London, with several signed performances for the deaf and hard of hearing. Linzi is partially deaf. I had done quite a lot of work, including a TV commercial, for the British Deaf Association and other charitable organizations.

As a result of this work I was presented with a Silver Heart in recognition of my contribution to showbusiness and children's charities by the Variety Club of Great Britain. They gave a lunch in my honour at the Grosvenor House Hotel. Jim Davidson was the compère and Virginia Bottomley – who was then Secretary of State for Health – was also present. Sir Tim Rice introduced me and said some lovely things. My family was very proud when I was presented with the Silver Heart. It was a wonderful day but I had been a little nervous. I'm fine when performing a character on stage. I am not so good at being myself in public. Which is why I nearly throttled Linzi.

During the run of *Barnum* I was in Bristol one night coming down the death slide at the end of the show. Unfortunately the rope sagged. I didn't have enough momentum to reach the stage, which meant I was left dangling over the orchestra pit. They had told me they were filming a commercial for the show and all I could think of was, 'This has messed up the TV commercial.' It was really embarrassing. It had never happened before and finally they managed to haul me on stage. It was very ungainly. At that point the audience applauded. I thought they were applauding my heroics. I glanced to my right and on walked Michael Aspel holding the famous Red Book. He said, 'Paul Nicholas – This Is Your Life.'

I had no idea. Then I put two and two together. Of course the cameras were there to film him coming on. It wasn't a commercial. I had been totally conned. Everyone else in the company knew except me. I didn't have a clue.

When I was at the height of my television fame with *Just*

Good Friends a few years earlier, I had always said to Linzi, 'If anybody ever contacts you from *This Is Your Life* the answer is "No!".' She said, 'Right.' I caught them out once. Somebody asked to speak to Linzi and it sounded like a very dodgy call. They pretended they were from a bookshop and I smelt it immediately. I couldn't think of anything worse than someone trotting out somebody I had not seen for a hundred years and saying, 'Do you remember Malcolm?'

I was not remotely interested in being the subject of *This Is Your Life*, but before I knew it I was backstage about to be whisked off to Bristol because they recorded it in a studio rather than on the stage. They'd had a suit brought in for me. My Irish dresser Trish McCauley knew, as did the cast. They'd all managed to keep it secret from me. They gave me time to have a shower and get changed. Then I walked out on to the set in front of an audience. There they were, all my family, friends and the rest of the cast.

Linzi had known about it since July. She had to keep this secret from the nosiest man in the world and she did. She had explained that I would not be comfortable in meeting blasts from the past, people I had not encountered for years. So it was a fairly civilized bunch like Jan Francis, Michael Ball, David Essex, Andrew Lloyd Webber, Victor Spinetti, Oliver Tobias, Elaine Paige, Wayne Sleep, Patty Boulaye, Belinda Lang, Dora Bryan, Robert Stigwood and my old employer, Screaming Lord Sutch.

This was my life and it was going well. I was also about to take control over my professional life and all because I decided to become a hired hand again. I agreed to do another tour of *The Pirates of Penzance*, once again playing the Pirate King. The reason why I have toured with *Pirates* so often is simply because it works. It was written in the late 1890s but our version was originally done in Central Park in New York by Joe Papp. Kevin Kline was the lead as the Pirate King and it was a great success and transferred to Broadway with Kline and Linda Ronstadt playing Mabel. When that production first came to Britain it had Tim Curry as the Pirate King and Pamela Stephenson as Mabel. George Cole played the Major General.

I had seen the Papp production at the Drury Lane Theatre and it was a fresh and lively version of a show that had been done in the same way for many years. Gilbert and Sullivan's original production had opened in Penzance and New York on the same night. It has fantastic charm, one of the reasons I enjoyed performing in it. It's great exercise and it allows me to be extremely silly. Above all when you take it out on a weekly tour around the country, people want to see it. Comparatively, it is not an expensive musical.

The tour began – but not with Michael Ball. This time a young actor called David Ian was to play the part of Frederick. David was from Ilford in London and had played Joseph in the *Amazing Technicolor Dreamcoat* and Rocky in *The Rocky Horror Show*. He was an excellent Frederick.

We hit it off instantly. We shared a similar sense of humour and had a lot of fun on stage together. We had a very good director called Chris Robinson. I thought David was a fine singer and sang it as well as Michael Ball. He took his dog, Penny, everywhere which I thought was nice. I met his mum and dad and liked them a lot.

I was restless on *Pirates* because I was again working for someone else. David, despite being younger – and I've always hated him for that – had the same frustrations. David turned 30 during the run. When you get to that age as an artist and you haven't quite made what you would consider an impression, you start to worry. You begin to think that you're never going to make it. Which is nonsense because you can make it at any age. My view is that you should never write anybody off.

Elaine Paige is a perfect example of that. Elaine was in the chorus of *Hair* and *Superstar*. She played Rita – one of Michael Crawford's girlfriends – in the musical *Billy*. Then, out of nowhere, she got *Evita* because ultimately she had the talent. If you'd have looked at Elaine Paige in *Hair* you wouldn't have believed that she could have played such a larger-than-life character as Eva Peron. If you love doing it, you should keep on trying because there are very few people who make it overnight and your time may come later in life.

The problem for David was not age. He was unsure of what he wanted to do. He liked the idea, like me, of not having to kowtow to anybody. To be your own man. Within the mix of what he was doing and what I was doing we talked over the idea of doing *Jesus Christ Superstar*. He came to me with the idea and I said, 'I'll do it if we produce it ourselves.' We became theatrical entrepreneurs.

Becoming a real life P. T. Barnum – a producer – in the theatre of the 1990s was not like an old-time Hollywood movie where you simply shout, 'Let's put on a show.' Although there were elements of it, both David and I were hands on about the idea. It was all down to us to make it work.

You have to take care of business first. We needed the rights to *Superstar* and luckily I had known David Land who had controlled them for Andrew Lloyd Webber and Tim Rice for many years. I said that we had an idea to do a concert version of *Jesus Christ Superstar* at the Blackpool Opera House. David Land granted us a licence for a one-off Sunday concert. Our whole focus became selling the concert.

We arranged for some top-class West End artists to be in it. David, who is a shrewd negotiator, was picking up the phone, talking to and booking the artists. He was fantastic at that. I said we needed to advertise on radio and I wrote the commerical. We needed a poster, so I designed it. We talked about all aspects of promotion and casting. The beauty of it was David would then pick up the phone and make it happen. I had found somebody at long last who was prepared to do what I couldn't do, which was organize it.

As a result of our efforts we sold out the Blackpool Opera House which is no mean feat, as it is has more than three thousand seats. We made a little bit of money. We thought, 'This is good.' So we thought we'd do another show. David Land agreed and we took an even bigger venue. The BIC in Bournemouth, which is about four thousand seats. It was another Sunday concert and another sell-out.

David Ian was working from his bedroom at his house. We sold out again. David had made a bit of money. I had made a bit of money. Suddenly David liked the idea of being a young producer, rather than being a theatrical second lead.

We decided to form a company and we called it 'Paul Nicholas and David Ian Associates'. And we started producing shows. We took a little office on a trading estate in Ilford in Essex. We did a little show in Bournemouth called *The Greatest Shows in Town* which was a compilation of songs from the musicals. It starred Rosemary Ford and Graham Bickley from *Bread*. We devised it, put it together and it worked very well and did a record breaking season.

We decided that we would try to do a nationwide concert tour of *Jesus Christ Superstar* and I was to perform on the five-week tour. It had been twenty years since I first performed it, so naturally we called it *The Twentieth Anniversary Concert Tour*. Again I phoned David Land and he granted us the rights to do the tour. I didn't pay myself any money on the tour – we were building a business – and it sold out places like the Glasgow Concert Hall, BIC, Bristol Colsten Hall, London's Fairfield Hall – big concert venues. It did very well and we were beginning to enjoy it. Everything was divided down the middle between David Ian and myself. I felt that the only way to go forward was to have a 50-50 relationship. I will always be grateful to David Land for giving us such a wonderful start. Sadly, he died in 1996. He was a wonderfully warm and funny man.

We wanted to move on as a company and considered doing *Tommy* as I had been in the movie. They were about to put it on in the West End so we had to let that one go. I came up with the idea of doing *Pirates* and David pointed out that it was a show not a concert. I pointed out that there was hardly any set, very little dialogue and that it was basically a light operetta. It would work very well in concert venues. When we put on dinner-jackets we could easily put on costumes. I must have been at my persuasive best.

We decided to do the show. No one had ever toured a West End show on a nightly basis in Britain. It was for five weeks and again I didn't pay myself anything. But I enjoyed myself and in the long term it paid off.The tour did very well and strangely enough *The Pirates of Penzance* tour did better than *Jesus Christ Superstar*. I thought it would be the other way around. Of course, we were not Cameron Mackintosh but we were developing as a company. With me holding the creative reins and with David's expertise on the day-to-day production, we were going places, we were a winning combination. David too was enjoying himself.

All the high-power business manuals tell you that the best business strategic planning has to look to the future. It is always a good question: what will you do next? We wanted to do a good revival but also a show that had not been seen on stage for a long time. I wanted a show, a *big* show, that we could get the rights to and produce as a tour. It's cheaper to launch a tour than to produce something for the West End. I was racking my brains and then it came to me: *Grease*. It was the show I really wanted to do.

Grease had continued to tour over the years in a small way but I knew from my youngest daughter Carmen that *Grease* was still incredibly popular. When they had sleep-over parties or kids just hung around the house, the video of *Grease* with John Travolta and Olivia Newton-John was a favourite. When they are little, they play *Mary Poppins*. When they are on hormone alert, it's *Grease*.

I just *knew* a revival of *Grease* was a winner. There was a snag. The rights to *Grease* didn't include four songs that were written specifically for the movie, 'Sandy', 'You're the One that I Want', 'Hopelessly Devoted' and 'Grease is the Word'. They, of course, were the key songs.

We felt that it was wrong to produce *Grease* without those songs, because people would expect to hear them. I thought Robert Stigwood, who had produced the film, might have the rights. I had not seen Robert since the late 1970s. He had yachted off and lived in Bermuda and New York. I was aware he had moved back to the Isle of Wight and bought a house there but I had not seen or spoken to him for years.

I went down to the Isle of Wight for lunch and as I hadn't seen Robert for such a long time, it was more of a social call. At the end of it I dropped in, 'Oh, by the way, I've got this little production company with a friend of mine called David Ian and we've done a few bits and pieces and we're thinking of doing *Grease*.' Robert's eyes fixed me with a look. He clearly wasn't happy. We had obviously chosen the right show. 'Any chance of helping us with the songs to *Grease*?'

He ummed and aahed and was bit non-committal. I said, 'It has been lovely seeing you, Bob, and take care and see what you can do for me on the songs. Thanks very much.'

We were going to go ahead without the songs, it didn't make any difference. I didn't hear anything from Robert and we started looking for people to star in it. One Sunday I suddenly got a call. Robert's on the phone. He said, 'I'm at Claridge's. Come over here, I want to speak to you.' I said, 'What about?'

He replied, 'I'm not telling you. Get over here now. It's urgent.'

I know Robert, when he goes, he goes. I jumped in a cab. We were in his lavish suite at Claridge's in the middle of Mayfair. He was straight to the point. He said, 'You've got the rights to *Grease* haven't you?' I said, 'Yeah. We're touring it.' He said, 'I want to do *Grease*.' Apparently he had been at Sydmonton with Andrew Lloyd Webber. He had met Cameron Mackintosh. He hadn't done anything in Britain for years, not since *Evita*. He found himself as the new boy back in town. His juices were flowing.

He had been speaking to Cameron and later they had talked about doing *Grease* together and they researched it a little bit and found that Paul Nicholas had the rights, which was going to mess them up and stop them doing it. We were in the way so Robert had to deal with me. Here am I an artist, not an entrepreneur. And as far as Robert is concerned, some-body without any credibility as a producer.

But we had the rights. He reiterated, 'I want to do *Grease*.' I thought for a second and answered, 'I would be delighted to do *Grease* with you, Robert.' David and I would've done the show without him but I thought it would be exciting to be involved with someone who would elevate the show to a different level. His experience gave the project a grandeur. I knew that when Robert did anything, he did it full on and properly and it would be a wonderful association for our new business.

I said, 'There is no problem, Bob. We'll do it fifty-fifty straight down the middle, all guns blazing.' We shook hands on it there and then at Claridge's. The celebrated whole bit. Robert does not stint on those things. When Robert travels from the Isle of Wight, he doesn't come by train or car. He comes by helicopter. I know, I've seen the expenses. He is Mr Producer.

We did the deal and talked about the theatre for the show. I said the Dominion would be a great theatre for it. It was always considered a bit of a dead duck. Nothing had ever really worked there. But the Dominion was a good-sized theatre with 2,000 seats. It was run by Apollo Leisure, a company I knew through *Barnum*. Mr Apollo Leisure is Paul Gregg, a straight-forward, terrific businessman who had built Apollo Leisure from nothing into one of the largest theatre groups in the country. He had been very good to me in *Barnum*. I thought he was somebody Robert could do business with.

We showed Robert the Dominion and he agreed it was a good venue. The choice of director was a little bit more difficult. The next question was who would play Danny and Sandy. I had played Danny with Elaine Paige at the New London Theatre. I knew the part and I felt the best person for it was someone that we had been thinking of prior to Bob's involvement. An actor called Craig McLachlan.

I had seen Craig on *Neighbours* in the Jason Donovan-Kylie Minogue era. I had watched him on the series and I thought he was very good-looking, had a naughty charm and a sense of comedy that the part of Danny required. He could also sing. I knew Craig had made records, although I was not sure how well he sang. I didn't think Danny would prove too difficult. The essence for me was that he was good-looking and funny.

I showed Robert some videos of him and we all thought that Craig would be the man for the job. We flew him from Australia to London. We all met at the Dorchester and lunch was laid on for Craig and his agent and the deal was struck that Craig would star. We booked Craig without hearing him sing or audition. He was so charming at that lunch. He was irresistible and obviously had the star quality needed.

We still had not found a Sandy, a director or a designer. A designer was key because the look of the show was extremely important. Robert and I have very similar taste and we both thought that the show should look very summery – not that clever on reflection. Very much like the movie. The problem with designers is that when you take on a designer you book them on the basis of reputation. You would not necessarily see their designs. Which means that you are never quite sure what they're going to come up with.

I knew a designer called Terry Parsons. I'd worked with him before on *Singin' in the Rain* and *Charlie Girl*. We interviewed him along with other top West End designers. Terry was the only one prepared to do a model of the design. Everyone was very sold on Terry's model and he got the job. The look of *Grease* had to be perfect for the show to work.

We still had no director. We decided to try and get Stephen Pimlott who had directed *Joseph*. He was flavour of the month at that time because *Joseph* had been a big success. He envisaged the production in the semi-round. This would have been very expensive and we felt it was unnecessary. So, instead we brought in David Gilmore, who was a very nice amenable man. We all liked him and he got the job. It was decided that Arlene Phillips, whom Robert didn't know but I did, would be the right choreographer for a show like *Grease*. Mike Dixon became the musical director and the costumes were by a terrific designer called Andreane Neofitou. She had designed *Les Misérables* and has tremendous taste.

We had everything else in place but we still didn't have the girl. The most difficult part of the show for Sandy is that she has to sing 'Hopelessly Devoted to You'. There's a point in the song where a lot of girl singers have to break from their normal chest voice into a head voice and it's technically quite a difficult moment in the song.

We saw a number of very good West End singers, some top-class girls, for that part and a great many of them couldn't make the change from chest to head successfully, without it breaking or sounding weak. Ideally, you wanted someone who could sing the whole song in chest voice.

There were other requirements. They also had to be pretty, seem demure and be able to act. That combination isn't easy to find. We were only two weeks from the first day of rehearsal and we still hadn't found a Sandy.

We heard on the grapevine that there was a singer called Debbie Gibson coming to Britain to do some TV. Debbie Gibson was then a very big pop singer in America. We managed to contact her manager, who was also her mother, and we managed to get her in to audition. She had a lovely warm quality, was extremely professional and hard-working, and she sang to die for. She was offered the part and she took it. We were then completely cast.

The first day that we put it on sale it did £100,000 of business. The great thing about it was that the business kept growing. We opened to one of the largest advances ever – over £4 million.

The belief that Robert brought to the show, for which I am indebted, is that you do not do things by half. Really terrific producers do things properly. When you get involved with someone like Robert, you learn about quality, you learn about style and about not being cheap. Robert is a tough businessman and Robert can be very hard to deal with but what he will never do is skimp on the show. It might not even work but it will be produced properly and you cannot say that of every producer.

Grease was capitalized at £2.5 million and although we opened with a £4 million advance that doesn't mean that the investors get their money back immediately. You have running costs every week and on a show like *Grease* at the Dominion, that is £130,000 a week. You have to pay rent to the theatre plus royalties to the creative team and the authors. There is a terrible myth that all artists believe, and which I believed until I started producing. That is that producers take all the money. The last person who gets paid is the producer.

On *Grease* we did have insurance. We were strong. We knew we had fantastic leads. We knew we had a terrific cast. We knew we had a great set. We knew we had a talented choreographer, director, musicians and a great venue. We had the capacity to play to over two thousand people every night.

My personal dilemma was how much of my own money to risk. There is a producers' share and an investors' share. I was obviously in on the producers' share, but there was also an investors' share. Did I want to invest? Robert and I could take outside investors or we could invest ourselves. We went for it. Robert likes a flutter. I'm not a gambler but I always remember James Goldsmith's motto, 'Never miss an opportunity.' I decided to take his advice.

I was playing for big stakes by my standards. I had been an artist, quite a successful one, but I had never been involved in a big production on the other side. I thought, 'This is an opportunity. I have got a piece of it. I want a bit more of this pie but I don't know how the show is going to go. I think it's a hit but I'm not Nostradamus. It was five months prior to the opening and we had to put our hands in our pockets to fund a £2.5 million production.

It is best to be prudent when investing in shows because one in seven doesn't get its money back. Even if that one in of seven runs for six months, it still may never get its money back because, although it could be breaking even every week, it might still not be recouping. *Sunset Boulevard* never got all its money back in London. It ran for two years and looked like a big success. And no one wants to be associated with a miss.

All this was in my mind as I was considering my further financial involvement. We had got the rights because we believed in it. I knew from Carmen how much kids liked it. In discos when they played 'You're the One That I Want' the boys lined up at one end of the dance floor and the girls lined up at the other and they'd do the number. I decided to have a punt.

I really fancied *Grease* and I put £500,000 in it. This was a lot for me. I think Robert put in about double that. Oscar told me I was mad. I believed in it and I hoped my hunch was correct.

We got Craig to do a record with Debbie and their 'You're the One that I Want' went into the charts after the show opened.

When the reviews came out, Robert and I went, 'Not bad.' Actually they were great, but I could already tell from the previews that we had a winner. Audiences were going mad. People were standing up and people are not stupid. You begin to smell a hit. You know when applause is genuine. You can tell. It's a different sound. As soon as the overture started and the audience heard the opening chords to 'Summer Nights', they were clapping along with the music. They wanted it and we gave it to them. At the end of the evening the audience was screaming for more. They still were in 1999. It remained a magnificent success. We were all thrilled with each other. We thought we were the best thing since sliced bread.

I was missing the emotional release of performing. I decided that I would like to do a big show. I had always wanted to do *Singin' in the Rain* because I had been to see it with my mum when I was a little kid. I had always hankered to do it. Harold Fielding controlled the rights to this along with some Americans but Harold was the one we needed to speak to. We got the rights and we went to see Apollo Leisure who had bought the set and costumes of *Singin' in the Rain* from Harold. Apollo Leisure have lots of theatres all over the country. As big provincial theatre owners they always need product.

They were happy to work with us on the staging of *Singin' in the Rain*. The slight problem, like the high wire in *Barnum*, was I could not tap dance. I could barely do a time step. But we had the rights and Tommy Steele, who had starred in it, would direct if he wanted to. We supposedly had the set and costumes. I would play the Gene Kelly part. It would be a big national tour staying at each venue about four or five weeks. Being such a big show to mount, we needed to stay in the venues longer to amortize the cost of the move. It was expensive. It required a lot of trucks to move the show from venue to venue.

I went to see Tommy in a show that he was doing at the time. A little tour called *What a Show* in which Tommy chronicled some of his past hits and talked to the audience. It was ever so good.

Tommy was wonderful. When I met him he said, 'When people meet me they do not know whether to shake my hand or give me a lump of sugar.' He has a great smile. It adds up to a lot of charisma. I asked if he would like to direct the show. He had directed the show at the London Palladium under Harold Fielding in the mid-1980s. It had been a big success. The rain scene was a priceless moment. Every show needs something that people look forward to. The way that they produced the famous rain scene in the movie on stage was clever.

It was the most famous scene in the film and the audience was fascinated to see how it was done. It was basically a huge shower. A set within a set. The water was pumped up from two water tanks below the stage. It would create the rain effect on the set and then drain away down to the water tanks below to be recycled again. It was important not to upset the crew because it was very easy for them to get their own back. I was always very mindful of the colour of the water. The only problem was that the set and costumes that we thought we had were non-existent and so not only did we have to build a new rain set, we also had to have new costumes made. It was a costly mistake and one that wasn't built into the budget for the show.

Nevertheless, I went out and fulfilled my boyhood dream of performing in a big show like *Singin' in the Rain*. Who doesn't' want to be Gene Kelly for a moment in their life? Tommy was very helpful to me and was a marvellous director. He did what most directors do not do: he ran the show every day. The worst thing about being in a big show is that by the time you have blocked the show you take so long to reach the end that you forget where you were at the beginning. By running the show every day – and not just the dialogue scenes – we all knew where we were. Even if we had got up to only two scenes, he would run it.

What normally happens with a show is you work it through, then do a couple of runs and then, the next thing you know, the curtain is going up. Often on the opening night, people are running around and cannot remember where they are and who they are supposed to be with. But Tommy kept running it so that everybody knew the running order of the show from day one, which I thought was a very useful tip. Tommy was also great to work with because he didn't try and project his performance on to mine.

My big problem had been learning to tap dance, which is one of the most difficult things in the world. It was strenuous and fiddly and hard work. I took two months prior to the rehearsals to learn to tap dance. But instead of learning to tap, which would have taken for ever, I decided to learn just the routines. The choreographer learned the routines, then taught them to a girl who then taught them to me. I was not learning to tap dance, I was learning to do the numbers, which was a lot easier. And after doing the show for a couple of years I could tap dance my way through the routines quite nimbly.

When I finished *Singin' in the Rain* I decided I would like to do slightly more serious stuff, a bit of straight work. I was asked to play King Arthur in *Camelot* – a powerful part in a wonderful musical. We did it at the Masonic Hall as part of the Covent Garden Festival. It was directed by Frank Dunlop and proved a very interesting process.

Bill Kenwright, who is a prolific producer, came to see me in *Camelot*. I let Bill know that I would be interested in doing some straight work. He offered me a play called *The Mysterious Mr. Love* written by Caroline Leach. It was about a real character called George Love. George was infamous for courting ladies, marrying them, drowning them in their baths and stealing their money. He did it three times before he was eventually caught.

It was set in the Edwardian period and Susan Penhaligon co-starred. We went to the Comedy Theatre and we were very well received and ran for three months. *The Mysterious Mr. Love* had all the elements that I loved because although it was a dark story, it was also a love story.

For some reason, although it was well reviewed, there was something about it that didn't work and unfortunately, if something isn't quite right with a play, it will never work. It was still a terrific play and wonderfully satisfying to think that two people could engage an audience for two hours. It showed me the power of good writing. We got close with *The Mysterious Mr Love* but not quite close enough and that was a shame.

It did give me a chance to show that I could do straight acting. That I didn't have to be Mr Musical all the time. *Mr. Love* worked well enough for me to be offered another couple of plays for Bill Kenwright. I co-starred with Chris Eccleston from *The Bill* in *Catch Me If You Can* and I also did a play called *The Dark Side* with Jenny Seagrove. Sadly, that was to prove an appropriate title for there were going to be some difficult times ahead.

12

Oscar Bows Out

I have a sort of obnoxious fighting charm but I'm a softie underneath.

– Oscar Beuselinck Sen, 1995

With Jenny, my father had another son, called Richard, in 1963. Oscar was a great guy in many, many ways but he was not the kind of parent who was 'hands on'. I think as a result Richard grew up without much confidence. He went to a good public school but that didn't make things easier for him.

It was great for me when he was born. Although I was eighteen years old I had always wanted a brother or sister. He came a little bit late for me but it was nice to think that there was somebody else there. Our nan gave him the same kind of treatment she had given me. She was good to him.

Richard played football and he was quite good. He excelled a bit on the sport front and I remember going with Oscar to this very smart school to see him play. Oscar could turn on the posh voice at the drop of a hat and was talking to a master while we were watching the football. Richard was 15 and Oscar was talking to the teacher about Richard's mock O levels. Removing his glasses he said, 'Look, I can assure you that although he may not do terribly well with his mocks, when it comes to the real thing, he'll piss it.'

That just made me die. It was another example of how embarrassing he could be, even then. He was the kind of guy who, if he met a good-looking woman, would remove his glasses so that she could get the full 'beauty' of his eyes. I took him on holiday to France with me in 1991. I'd hired a villa in Grasse in the South of France and it was wonderful for about three days but then, of course, he started to irritate me. I remember him taking his glasses off one day to my then three-year-old daughter and saying, 'Carmen. Do you think I look better with or without my glasses?'

He was the sort of man who would get my elder daughter Natasha to ride around in the front of the car with him because he would rather have her next to him than my elderly mother. The great thing about Oscar was that he was aware of all his idiosyncrasies. It didn't, however, stop him behaving that way.

He was very interested in my business. He was forever asking me for tickets and people always told me that he was very proud of what I had managed to do. I was proud of him. I always wanted to emulate him. He was a very successful lawyer. You always want to please your parents. Our telephone conversations were like a tennis match. We would invariably end up screaming at each other.

Oscar had been married three times – to my mother, to Jenny and to a lady called Ann Wadsworth. Oscar used to call her 'Worthwads'. Ann didn't stand for any of Oscar's nonsense and they too remained good friends. His second wife, Jenny, had married a man called Johnny Russell. Oscar had known him from the Jack Hylton days. Johnny Russell used to produce for Jack. I was always very happy to talk to Johnny. He was a nice man and we talked about the theatre. He was very knowledgeable.

Oscar had a flat in London. He had a very enjoyable job as a consultant for Davenport Lyons, a prestigious law firm in Savile Row. And at weekends he would go down to the house that he owned in Folkestone where Jenny and Johnny Russell also lived. They would go away on holidays together. It suited him perfectly. He had someone to do his washing and cooking

'There's a sucker born every minute.' As the legendary showman P. T. Barnum. Playing him started me thinking about producing musicals.

A high wire Gotcha! Michael Aspel caught me with the big red book for *This is Your Life* during the run of *Barnum*.

The Screaming Lord has the last laugh: Sutch presenting me with my leopardskin 'Savages' costume on *This is Your Life*.

'Come follow the band …' *Barnum. (Above)*

'Fit as a Fiddle': tap-dancing with Tony Howes in *Singin' in the Rain. (Above)*

Tommy Steele directing me in the film sequences for *Singin' in the Rain. (Right)*

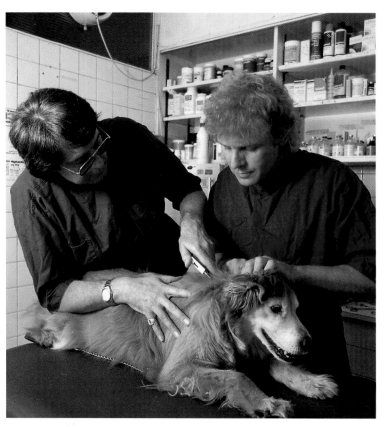

They say never work with kids and animals – I appeared with both in *Close to Home*. Learning the ropes with vet Nigel Norris. *(Left)*

As bankrupt Neil Walsh. They called the series *Bust* but it did very well for ITV pulling in more than 11 million viewers – my follow-up to *Just Good Friends*. *(Below)*

With my partner
David Ian, the
legendary Harold
Fielding and
Tommy Steele
during preparations
for *Singin' in the
Rain*. *(Above)*

In New York with Robert Stigwood holding court
in grand style over breakfast. *(Above)*

'Perfectamundo Aaay.' Henry Winkler, 'The
Fonz', and I at the launch of *Happy Days* the
musical in Manchester in 1999. *(Left)*

A couple of my favourite performers: Debbie Gibson and Craig McLachlan as Sandy and Danny in *Grease*. (*Above*)

Adam Garcia and the cast of *Saturday Night Fever* at the London Palladium. (*Below*)

As the Mysterious Mr. Love at the Comedy Theatre with Susan Penhaligon in the background. *(Above)*

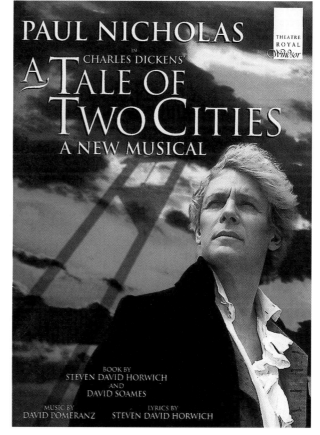

'It is a far, far better thing that I do, than I have ever done ...' As Sydney Carton. *(Right)*

Getting everyone to smile at the same time wasn't easy: the family, summer 1999.
Front row (left to right): Oscar, Natasha, Amber, Carmen, Bobby and Joseph.
Back row (left to right): Alexander, Linzi, Ruby, myself and Mum.

and he had people to talk to. He would visit us in Highgate, eat a rice pudding, read the newspaper, fall asleep and, as he was leaving, if you were lucky, he would nod and say hello to his grandchildren.

Unfortunately, Johnny Russell had cancer. He was incredibly brave about it. He knew that he was dying and yet he was always courteous and stood up when my mother and Linzi entered the room. He seemed to me very stoical and didn't complain about his condition.

Oscar still had a soft spot for Jenny although he had a girlfriend called Corrine, another lovely lady. She was very attractive and he would take her with him to various showbusiness events. He was still very much in touch with what was going on and had an instinctive feel for the theatre.

Poor Johnny Russell died and I believe Oscar was genuinely sad to see him go. They had known each other for fifty years. Johnny Russell certainly had the measure of Oscar.

Oscar was happy. He was still working. Richard had married Martina, an Irish girl, and Oscar had a beautiful baby granddaughter called Maria. He could still walk about the office, drive his partners mad and open their mail. He could go down and see Jenny at weekends. Everyone was in their place.

Oscar telephoned me and for once we didn't have the usual row. He had been away and I had not spoken to him for two weeks. It was nice to hear from him. I told him I had a bad back and he recommended a cure. It was an unusually nice conversation.

The next day, I was alone in my garden in Highgate. Linzi, my mum and Carmen were on holiday in France. The phone rang. It was my brother Richard and he said, 'Hello, Paul. I don't know how to tell you this but I think Oscar may have died.'

I said, 'What do you mean?'

He replied, 'Well, they found the body of a man on the Leas. They think it's Oscar.'

Oscar used to love walking on the Leas in Folkestone. I got a terrible feeling in my stomach. I thought, 'It *is* Oscar.'

After his Sunday morning breakfast he had gone out to get the newspapers, helped himself to his favourite Belgian chocolates and while Jenny was cooking his lunch he decided to go for a walk. While walking on the Leas, he had a massive heart attack. It was the end of a remarkable life.

The next evening, I was appearing at Windsor in *The Mysterious Mr Love*. Oscar's death hadn't yet hit me. Oscar was 77 years old and when your parents get to that age, you half expect the worse. Oscar was very philosophical about death. I wasn't sure how I was feeling. I had to work. I got through the first half of the play. In the second half the character I was playing has a long speech reminiscing about his father. It is a sensitive and well-written speech and was not dissimilar to my thoughts about my own father. I began the speech and it seemed to me that I was talking about Oscar. I became very emotional and the floodgates opened. I began to cry. Susan Penhaligon was very, very kind to me and helped me get through it. I suppose my crying wasn't inappropriate for the scene. After the show, Sheila Ferguson – a singer who had once been in the Three Degrees – came back to see me. She told me how much she had enjoyed the play and how she had been particularly moved by the speech. She said, 'How do you do it? How do you cry like that every night?' Being the old ham that I am, I didn't tell her.

I had to arrange the funeral. It could have been in Folkestone but so many friends of Oscar's – from showbusiness and the legal profession – wanted to be there. So we held it at Golders Green Crematorium. We had an overflowing church. Timothy Dalton and Richard Harris came along to pay their respects. Brian Wadsworth and my solicitor Barry Shaw – a close friend and colleague of Oscar's – gave readings. Everybody was very kind and told me how proud he was of me. We talked about how full of life he was and how we all missed him.

Oscar had left instructions that if there were to be a memorial service after his death, he would like it held at St George's Church at Queen Square just three hundred yards from Milman Street, Holborn, where Oscar grew up and where at 14 he had become an altar boy. So with the help of Philip Conway of Davenport Lyons, on 3 November 1998 a memorial service was held. Again the church was packed. Two very famous lawyer friends of Oscar's, did the readings. George Carman, QC read one and the actor John Thaw – well-known as *Kavanagh QC* – read the other.

A brilliant young violinist called So Ock Kim played one of Oscar's favourite pieces, Massenet's 'Meditation', accompanied by my son Alexander on the piano. Tributes were paid by Jarvis Astaire, former Deputy Chairman of Wembley Stadium, Robert Stigwood, Peter Ash and Arthur Davidson QC, who recalled, 'I must say up here I do feel a sense of nerves and fear because I'm thinking, "What would Oscar's reaction be to seeing me up here?" I know what the reaction would be. He would say "What have you got him up there for? I could have got somebody much better than him. I could have got George Cole if you'd asked." And then of course he would have reacted in a predictable way. He would have shouted, he would have objected and then ultimately, offered his resignation.'

Finally, Peter Ash, who had known and worked with Oscar for over forty years told of Oscar's inability to do *The Times* crossword. 'I remember one clue which he did which impressed him greatly. It was a five-letter word and it said, "He started with nothing but then left his mark", and of course the answer was "Oscar". Oscar started with nothing and he left his mark. I think that's an appropriate epitaph for him.'

Oscar received many obituaries, including two half-pages in *The Times* and the *Telegraph*, which is very unusual for a lawyer. Ned Sherrin gave his memorial service a wonderful review in the *Oldie*. I'm sure Oscar would have been delighted.

Oscar was a big part of my life and is irreplaceable. I loved him very much and I think about him a great deal. Always fondly rather than sadly.

13

A Star is Born

Stigwood wanted to call the film *Saturday Night* but we had already written 'Night Fever' so we compromised on *Saturday Night Fever.*

– Robin Gibb, March 1978

I always enjoyed a turbulent, see-saw relationship with my father, but he was a man to listen to. One piece of advice could not have been clearer: 'Do not put your own money in a show.'

Well, I had certainly ignored him when we produced *Grease* and here I was doing it again with *Saturday Night Fever*. I had money in the show under the auspices of our production company, Paul Nicholas and David Ian Associates, as well as my own separate investment. I was using my own money and the odds against getting it back were long. It's a highly risky business. Here was I, in for a penny ... in for a million pounds. 'Character building', I told myself.

It was a big commitment. Obviously, I was very keen to be as hands on as possible about it. When you are dealing with a man like Robert Stigwood who, like all great producers, has a total self-belief, most of the time it's all right. Some of the time it isn't. I like to keep up with the latest shows and movies, learning what and who is popular. It helps keep you in touch as a producer and as a performer. It's certainly an ethic that rewarded me with *Saturday Night Fever*. My taste is simple: I like a good story with great music. If the story and music work then you have a chance. If they don't, no matter how hard you dress it up, your chances of making the show work are very slim. What we had with *Fever* was a good story, great songs and a well known title. Hopefully a hit!

To my mind our problem was structural. A script for a movie is quite different from that for a musical. What we had to do was adapt the movie to the stage. The problem was that the movie had never been a 'musical'.

Saturday Night Fever is about a guy who works in a paint store. His only chance to excel and be a star is on the dance floor. What we needed to do was to make sure that the story of Tony, Annette and Stephanie – the love triangle – could be told clearly. In the film most of the songs are sensitively placed and work very well as background to the scenes. The positioning of the songs and dialogue was the key to making the stage musical work.

Arlene had a wonderful track record as a choreographer. She had worked on Andrew Lloyd Webber's *Starlight Express* and Michael Flatley's *Lord of the Dance*, as well as choreographing more than a dozen movies. But she had never directed a West End show before. Robert thought she was the right choice to direct *Fever*, particularly as the show was music- and dance-driven. The dancing would give the show its identity. There are well over sixteen genuine hit songs; most shows have only one or two. What we now needed was the star.

We were looking for someone who looked as good as John Travolta, someone who could sing the Bee Gees songs and, more importantly, someone who could dance. You might think that given the vast pool of talent throughout the country, performers would come flooding through the door. They didn't. After all these years, that still surprises me.

Luckily, in 1994 I had been at a Variety Club dinner at the Grosvenor House and part of the cabaret was from a show called *Hot Shoe Shuffle* which was playing at the Queen's Theatre in the West End. It was a tap-dancing show that had originated in Australia and was very good. There were about a dozen dancers. At the end of the line of dancers I noticed a very young, more than usually handsome, dark-haired guy, who was a fantastic tapper. We were auditioning people for *Grease* at the time and I thought he had star potential. I had my two daughters with me and they were both seriously impressed by him. He was, as my teenage daughter would say, extremely 'fit'.

This was my first encounter with Adam Garcia. What struck me about him was that he looked so much like John Travolta. He really stood out. He had the same quality as Travolta – vulnerability and boyish charm. He was clearly a brilliant dancer. We were focused on *Grease* at that time, but I knew *Fever* was on the cards and I was thinking ahead.

I talked to Robert and David Ian and suggested Adam try out for the role of Doody in *Grease*. I said I felt that he also had the potential to play Tony Manero, the Travolta part in *Saturday Night Fever*, when we finally got round to producing it. We asked him in for an audition but when he arrived I was somewhat surprised. Instead of seeing this sexy Travolta type with shiny black hair, in shuffled this kid of about 18 in an old overcoat, wearing glasses and looking about twelve. I had called everyone in for this audition and when Adam sang he didn't sing terribly well. When he read for the part of Doody he didn't project. He was laid back and rather inexperienced but there was something about him that was different. A couple of years earlier he had been studying science at Sydney University and surfing in his spare time. He was more Beach Boys than Bee Gees.

Robert Stigwood, like me, also saw Adam's potential. Although he hadn't sung brilliantly, he'd sung well enough and he got the part of Doody. *Grease* helped Adam to grow as a performer. We were by now preparing the auditions for *Saturday Night Fever*. Adam had become number one in everyone's mind to play Tony Manero. He knew this and had worked with Arlene prior to auditions. He had gone to Brooklyn to work on his accent and lose his natural Australian twang.

In September 1997 we all turned up at the Cambridge Theatre in London to watch Adam Garcia audition for the part of Tony Manero. He failed to impress. He gave a poor audition. Yes, he looked fantastic. Yes, his dancing was good, but Arlene had doubts about his determination to be the Tony Manero she wanted. As she put it, did he have the kind of real punch and expertise that the show would require? His singing was not his strongest suit and his acting, although it was OK, didn't reach beyond the front row.

Adam's first report card as Tony Manero was 'could do better' and we were worried. I suppose, subconsciously, I was expecting him to walk on stage and just wow everybody, myself included. Adam left everybody with a certain amount of doubt. Arlene had great doubts, David Ian – my partner – had huge doubts. I believed that he needed further work and had the potential within him to succeed, as did Robert.

I suggested – after much discussion – that we should work on him and bring him back at a later date to re-audition. At the same time, let's be practical. Let's keep searching for a Tony Manero.

Immediately there was a problem. Arlene couldn't work with Adam because she was contracted to go off and work on the show *EFX*, the Michael Crawford extravaganza at the MGM Hotel in Las Vegas. We needed Adam ready within four weeks and Arlene was committed. I suggested we use a director that I had worked with to prepare Adam but Robert wasn't happy with that. He thought bringing someone else in would undermine Arlene. So he asked me to do it instead.

I had a new role and I was delighted with it. I could not be more hands-on. It was like being in one of those Judy

Garland-Mickey Rooney 1940s movies when all the kids jump up and down and decide to put on a show. The difference for me was that this was very serious show*business*.

I set up a series of daily rehearsals for three weeks. I arranged for Adam to work on three numbers and three scenes. Although Adam's audition wasn't fantastic, when he sang 'Night Fever' it had worked. One of my fears prior to Adam's audition, was that anybody other than the Bees Gees singing the songs from *Saturday Night Fever* might sound ordinary. The Bee Gees' falsetto voices were so identifiable. What became clear to me at Adam's first audition and what I found very exciting was that it sounded perfectly natural for those songs to be sung without falsetto. That was a big moment and I said to myself, 'This is going to work. Musically this is going to work.'

But from then on my job was to help Adam become Tony Manero. The potential was all there; he just had to find it. I understood Adam and what he was going through. When you are a young performer, you can fool yourself into believing you are being real and natural. The thing Adam lacked above all else was projection, both with singing and acting and, to a lesser extent, with his dancing. It might have sounded great in his head but we needed to get it as well.

We started rehearsing. We worked on all facets of his performance. We started at ten in the morning and worked through until four. A long physical day for him and for me. I wanted him to convince everyone else and Adam himself that he could play the part.

We worked on his singing and his acting. I kept telling him, 'Adam this is a fantastic opportunity for you. Big opportunities come along once in a lifetime. It's very important that you get this part. I think you're right for the part. I know that Robert believes you're right for the part. However, *you* have to know you're right for the part. Arlene certainly needs to be convinced because she's going to have to work with you.' It was a psychological thing with him. I don't think he really believed that he had it in him to play the role. I think there was a lack of self-belief. The part had been created by John Travolta and it was a lot to live up to.

The big day arrived and they were all going to be there: Robert, Arlene, Phil Edwards – the musical supervisor – David Ian and Robert's right-hand man, Patrick Bywalski, Arlene's assistants, Tony Edge and Karen Bruce. All the creative people were there to see Adam re-audition. I couldn't sit still. I was very nervous.

We got to the Cambridge Theatre early. We rehearsed and we rehearsed and even as Robert was walking through the door with Arlene, we were still at it. I asked Robert to wait outside. I was beginning to lose it. This had become an 'us-and-them situation' and there was no way we were going to lose. It was a bit like being a boxing trainer. I heard myself saying ridiculous things like, 'Go on my son. Knock 'em out.' If he hadn't, I certainly would have done!

Adam came on stage. I was thinking, 'Be strong. Be positive. Just do it.' I sat at the back of the theatre. I was too nervous to sit with the others. We put the backing tape on to 'Stayin' Alive' and he came out and he sang it. He bowled them over. A complete transformation had taken place. I was starting to fill up. I could sense that the audience, even though there were only eight of them, were getting excited too.

He did a couple of dialogue scenes which worked well and then 'Night Fever'. He was brilliant. They were in shock as to how much Adam had improved in three weeks. I was completely and utterly thrilled. Robert was so knocked out that he came up to me and said, 'You've done a fantastic job. I want you to co-direct the show. In fact I'm going to get Arlene to ask you now.' I think the excitement had got to him.

Arlene took me aside and said how impressed she was and would I co-direct the show, and I said, 'I think you need to go away and think about this. I think we are all riding on a high.' Which we were. We were all so relieved that Adam had shown that he could do it. I didn't want to be the co-director. I believed that Arlene should be the sole director. It was her gig. Robert embraced me. He felt the problem was solved. I was relieved. David Ian was more convinced, although not totally.

The only thing that was bothering me now was the script. Only weeks before the show was to open, it still wasn't right. Nan Knighton and Arlene had worked very hard but I still didn't think it was quite right. I was very keen to get the structure right and put back Norman Wexler's original film script. I said to Robert, 'I don't want to co-direct. What I want to do is work on the script because I don't think it's quite working.' He knew the script wasn't perfect and so off I went to work with Arlene on the structure of the script. We brought in numbers like 'Tragedy', which weren't in the original film. I found the process fascinating.

I think Robert Stigwood is a great producer but we didn't always see eye to eye. On occasions we'd have stand-up, screaming rows on various points on *Saturday Night Fever*. I was willing to be strong because I had a huge investment in the show and I was protecting myself. That was the bottom line.

The problem with producing shows is that you are dealing with so many egos. People don't tell the truth. People protect their own position rather than the product. My view was you mustn't lose sight of the product. You don't manoeuvre for the next job because if you mess this job up there won't be a next job.

That was another reason I worked so hard with Arlene to get the script right for *Saturday Night Fever*. After many weeks of working, we finally reached a point where we believed, 'This will work'. With that confidence, we concentrated on the presentation of the show. Robert was very keen on the London Palladium but I had doubts. It is an expensive venue in terms of rent and staffing and has 2,300 seats. The Dominion, where we were presenting *Grease*, seated about the same number but I had always felt *Grease* was a more certain hit. I knew from my youngest daughter – who watched the *Grease* video constantly – that there was an instant market. She was not so interested in *Saturday Night Fever*.

I had to admire Robert's confidence. He insisted, 'I want the Palladium.' I thought he'd overcooked it. So did my partner. The Palladium became free. *Oliver* was ending its run. We set an opening date. We had a theatre. We had a star. We had a script.

All we had to do was sell tickets. How? We needed a logo. The first design we were offered was a drawing of a man wearing a white suit in the famous Travolta pose. It wasn't very good. It didn't work. I asked the designer Bob King to incorporate the famous pose, using the letters of *Saturday Night Fever*. It took more than thirty designs to get it right. The first thing the public sees is the poster and I had learned from Robert that attention to detail is vitally important in any enterprise.

We still didn't have a female lead. Then out of nowhere we found a wonderful Australian girl called Anita Louise Combe. She became Stephanie Mangano.

I wanted to do a workshop on the basis that if it didn't work in a room with six actors, it wasn't going to work on the stage. Forget costumes and scenery. Robert doesn't like workshops but Arlene and I thought it was important, particularly with a new show. He relented. We wanted to see how the script developed and as soon as they started the first number, we could see it working.

Audiences are no longer willing to accept a 1960s approach

with modern musicals – lengthy scenes followed by a song. People are used to flipping TV channels. It was vital to us to ensure that they didn't get bored, that there was a sustained pulse running through the show. So we kept things moving. In the first workshop we could see that it would work.

Robert agreed to a second workshop and this time we were able to use the actors that were going to be in the show. After this second workshop, we really knew we had something.

We were into rehearsals. After a week of rehearsals, I went to see a runthrough of the first act with the full cast. I had never been so excited in my entire life. It had worked. The dialogue was underscored and the dance was integrated into the songs. I thought, 'Magic.' And went berserk. I hugged everyone.

We were completely thrilled with what Arlene had done. I said to her, 'Adam's wonderful. The show's wonderful. You're wonderful!' It was a great moment for her because here was someone telling her that it was better than OK. It was great! It filled her with great confidence. Robert announced to the entire company, 'It's a smash!'

We had to make sure the promotion was right. We needed as much profile for the show and exposure for Adam as we could get. We found out who the PR people behind the Spice Girls were. It was a company called Brilliant. We took them on, which allowed us to market the show in a more contemporary way than was normal. David Ian remained a little nervous but that is part of David's careful nature. His caution is an asset.

Another problem emerged. One of the girls playing a featured part wasn't working out. She had a great voice and looked terrific but she hadn't the experience required for the role. We wanted her understudy to replace her, which is what happened. It was a tough decision and Robert had to make it. To the girl's great credit she stayed with the show in another role. That was the most heartbreaking moment during rehearsals.

David and I went to the first technical rehearsal. This is when sets, costumes, lights and sound are put together for the first time. You block the scene, run it and move on to the next scene. It's like watching a bad performance in slow motion and can be very dispiriting. It's no way to judge a show. We watched it from the gods because I wanted to watch it quietly. As the 'disco spaceship' was refusing to land for the third time, David leaned across and said, 'How much have you got in this?' It was a wind-up and irritating, but the word on *Saturday Night Fever* at that point was iffy. I was on the hook for much more than anybody else. Next to Robert, I was the highest investor.

I remembered what my old man always said to me, 'Never put your own money in a show.' Any decent producer would always use other people's money. Everybody always tells you that. You limit the risk with lots of investors (angels). They all get a piece and you pick up the producer's share. One thing that I have learned from Robert – who is a gambler – is that if you believe in something, you go for it. My old man's advice conflicted with that. I believed in *Grease* and then in *Saturday Night Fever*. You don't get that many opportunities to get involved in something you think will really go. *Grease* was one of them. I'd put half a million quid of my own money in *Grease*, and it had paid off. It was a huge success. I thought we could do the same with *Saturday Night Fever* and, although the amount of money was so much more, it wasn't as if I had never put a big bundle on the red before. Some of Robert's self-belief had rubbed off on me. He does have that effect on you.

Robert Stigwood is a tough nut but I don't think anybody in showbusiness has quite encompassed what he has in the entertainment industry. Sir Cameron produces great musicals, Lord Lloyd Webber writes brilliant musicals and Lord Lew Grade was a brilliant impresario but there hasn't been anyone in the last fifty years who's been so diverse in the entertainment field as Robert. I have tremendous admiration for him. Figures like him never lose that total self-belief that separates the men from the boys. When everyone else is falling apart and looking for support, people like Robert are still going forward.

Saturday Night Fever opened on 5 May 1998. The streets around the Palladium were jammed. I had hired a large car for myself and my family and we couldn't get near the theatre. It was bedlam. I have never seen so many photographers, TV crews and fans waiting for the many stars and celebrities to arrive for the show. It was a real event. It took us fifteen minutes to walk the hundred yards to the theatre. I ushered my family into a side room reserved for the producers. We were very grateful for a quiet drink.

When we took our seats in the auditorium, I began to feel very nervous. Not only for myself but for the cast. I knew how they would be feeling. Slowly the theatre filled up. There was a tremendous air of expectation. The lights dimmed and the orchestra started to play the overture. As the overture climaxed a spot hit the centre of the stage and there was Adam standing in the classic Travolta pose. There was an enormous cheer from the audience and as the opening riff of *Saturday Night Fever* began to play, I thought, 'It's a winner!'

The next morning the reviews appeared. They were mixed. The good ones were excellent and the not-so-good ones were OK: '*Fever* is still hot stuff, any night of the week' (*The Times*); '*Fever*'s got real flare' (*Sun*); 'A sensational night out' (*Daily Mirror*). There were others but by now Adam's recording of 'Night Fever' was climbing the charts and there had been enough promotion and publicity to give the show great profile.

Our two weeks of previews had been sold out and we had

the most important thing of all: we had great word of mouth. The phones in the box-office didn't stop ringing and they had to take on extra staff to cope with the demand. *Fever* was a smash and was set for a long run.

Robert, David and I had had a tough year producing the show and frankly we needed a break from each other. When you are in a cauldron of pressure as we were, it can be a very testing time. However, we'd done it. We had a show that we believed in and felt proud of. At the end of the day, that's the only thing that mattered.

Epilogue
An Actor's Lot

It is a far, far better thing that I do, than I have ever done; it is a far, far better rest, that I go to, than I have ever known.

> – Sydney Carton in Charles Dickens's
> *A Tale of Two Cities*

*G*rease and *Saturday Night Fever*, although great successes, had one thing in common, they were revivals. *Saturday Night Fever* less so, because we had adapted it from a film. Nevertheless, the show had a ready-made score. I wanted to do something new. I had never been involved with a musical from day one: from the originating idea through to the finished product on stage.

With that in mind, I spoke to a friend of mine David Soames. David is a very active writer. He wrote the musical *Time* which starred Cliff Richard. As well as writing on his own, he co-wrote with two Americans: Steven David Horwich, a very talented script writer and lyricist and David Pomeranz a wonderful singer who also wrote the hits; 'Trying to Get the Feeling' and 'The Old Songs' for Barry Manilow and 'I Believe In Fairytales' for Cliff.

David Soames had brought me an earlier musical that they had written and, although I wasn't taken with the show, I liked the songs. So I asked David to adapt a musical from an existing story, book or play. I asked him to put this to Pomeranz and Horwich and see if they could come up with something. This was to be the beginning of a long process, not helped by the fact that they lived six thousand miles away in Los Angeles.

207

The 'something' they came up with was *A Tale Of Two Cities* by Charles Dickens. I liked the idea. So I bought the book. The story takes place during the French Revolution and moves between Paris and London.

Dr Manette, a French doctor, attends a poor family and becomes aware that his patients are the victims of maltreatment and mortal wounding by the Marquis de Evrémonde. To secure his silence, the doctor is imprisoned in the notorious Bastille prison for 18 years. When he emerges, the demented doctor is brought to England by his long-lost daughter Lucie Manette. Charles Darnay, the nephew of the Marquis, can no longer stand the cruelty of the French aristocracy and goes to England where he meets and marries Lucie. At the height of the French Revolution, Darnay travels to Paris to attempt a rescue of his former teacher Gabelle, who is accused of serving the nobility. He is himself arrested, imprisoned and sentenced to death. At the last minute Darnay is smuggled out of prison by Sydney Carton, a dissolute English barrister whom he closely resembles and who is devoted to Lucie. Carton then takes Darnay's place on the scaffold, adding self-sacrifice to this poignant tale of suffering. Dickens own verdict on the book was, 'The best story I have written'.

A Tale of Two Cities has the rambling quality of a modern-day soap opera. What struck me, however, was the similarity between the end of the book and *Jesus Christ Superstar*. Jesus martyrs himself as does Dickens's hero Sydney Carton. I fancied the part of Carton. I asked Pomeranz and Horwich to put a couple of ideas on tape, which they did. I liked what I heard and requested more material, suggesting that when it was completed, we fly them over to play the songs and we would take it from there. They agreed.

Three months later David Ian and myself met the writers at my house to listen to what had now become six songs. As Pomeranz finished singing the last song, Carton's 'What a

Man May Do', I looked at David Ian. He looked at me, we both had tears in our eyes. Mine were brought on by the beauty of the music, David was tearful because he could see that I was about to spend the company's money. We commissioned them to write a full-scale musical and they flew back to America.

Three months later, the tapes of the completed musical arrived. Both David and I decided to listen to them separately. They had written, at my request, a 'sung-through' musical in the style of *Les Misérables*. It had very little dialogue. As I listened, I had a sinking feeling. David Pomeranz is a terrific song-writer, but telling the story through song rather than dialogue takes twice as long and recitative sung narrative is a very difficult musical form to pull off. It's important that, musically, it's melodic enough for the audience to remain receptive. If they switch off, they don't get the story. I found some of David's recitative rather angular and not easy on the ear. Because the story shifts between London and Paris with many different characters, half of whom are French, the plot is very involved and confusing. I called David Ian and he felt the same way. Back to the drawing board and another year of faxes, tapes and telephone calls between London and Los Angeles. Indeed this was a tale of two cities.

Part of our deal with the writers meant we were under obligation to do a workshop and after two years of work, we all needed to have a look. So we booked twelve actors and a rehearsal room in London. After a week of rehearsals, they presented the musical to David, the writers and myself. After only five minutes I got that sinking feeling again. I thought this isn't working. We hadn't really solved the problems. The recitative was still hard to listen to and the story still wasn't clear. Yes, the songs were great but that wasn't enough. David and I were a little dispirited. We had employed David Gilmore – the director of *Grease* – to direct it and give it shape. He'd done the best he could but it still didn't work. David Ian wanted to let it go. Quite rightly. We had invested a lot of company money in the project and were about to lose our option. It would have involved further expense.

It was Christmas 1996 and the writers again returned to America. Everyone was a bit depressed. I still couldn't let it go. I felt that we needed a fresh approach to the musical. So I called Bob Tomson who had directed *Blood Brothers* and *The Mysterious Mr Love*. Bob is extremely thorough and one of the hardest working directors I've ever worked with. I played him the workshop tape and gave him the history of the show. He wanted to be involved. He got in touch with the boys and, once again, it was phones, faxes and tapes. Bob and I would review the work together and suggest changes. I had no contract with the writers, it was all done on trust. The show had by now become a traditional book musical. Slowly it got better and better.

At last it reached the point where I felt confident enough to take it to Bill Kenwright. Bill is a marvellous producer who does everything from *Joseph and the Amazing Technicolor Dreamcoat* to plays and films. He's always willing to give new writers a chance and keeps a lot of actors gainfully employed. He also runs the Theatre Royal in Windsor, an opportunity, I hoped, for a try out. I didn't play him the workshop tape, I played him the six songs. He liked them and the idea of the musical. I suggested that they play him the whole score. He agreed.

I flew Pomeranz and Horwich over from the States and together with Bob Tomson and David Soames, they played Bill the musical on a piano in his office. With a few reservations, Bill loved it. A date was set to open at the Theatre Royal in Windsor – July 1998.

Although *A Tale of Two Cities* has an epic quality, it is essentially a love story. The question was whether to do it big or small – the Theatre Royal has 600 seats. Bill had the answer,

'We do it small, sixteen actors and a six-piece band.' Small didn't mean cheap. Bill had to invest £250,000 on set and costumes for a six week run at Windsor, on the chance that he might have a show at the end of it. He had little hope of getting his money back. Not many producers do that. Bill did.

At last we were into rehearsal and, guess what, I got the part of Sydney Carton. Well, I knew him inside out! I was thrilled for the writers and Bob. They had stuck with the show when at times it seemed it would go under. They rarely got upset or grand and were always willing to try a different approach for the good of the show. They never lost sight of their goal. I think the show has a great future. We have already played the 1998–99 Christmas season at the Alexandra Theatre in Birmingham and there are plans for a further tour, followed by a West End run.

For me, nothing will compare with that opening night in Windsor. After six years of trying, we'd finally got it on. It was up there living and breathing on the stage of the Theatre Royal with a real paying audience out front. The show was very well received and I felt so proud to have been a part of it.

In the final scene of the musical, as Sydney Carton is led up the steps of the guillotine to meet his fate, he delivers the famous lines that conclude the book: 'It is a far, far better thing that I do, than I have ever done; it is a far, far better rest that I go to, than I have ever known.' I think he spoke for all of us.

There is a very fine line between something that works and something that doesn't. It's not enough to have a good show. It has to be a great show! It's very difficult to go into a West End theatre with a brand new show and expect to have it dead right. It's almost impossible. We made a few small changes to *Saturday Night Fever* between the previews and opening night. You can tinker with a show, but it is very wearing for the cast to try and do more. After all they are performing at night, which leaves a limited amount of time during the day. I would always recommend workshopping a show before you spend £4 million on it. It takes a very brave man not to. If it doesn't work in one room with six people and a piano, it won't work anywhere – no matter how many millions it costs.

As a performer, you receive great satisfaction from making people happy, be it on TV, in a film or on the stage. There's nothing like the buzz of performing in front of a live audience. I am basically a shy person and performing gives me a tremendous release. I'm not a great party animal. My motto is: 'Why do I need to go to a party? Where else can I can get dancing, music, girls and always be the centre of attention?'

The only way I can get that total satisfaction is to do a musical because if it is any good it will contain elements of every discipline: dance, songs, humour and drama. I think it's very therapeutic to be in your late forties learning to walk a wire, juggle or tap dance. It shows that the only limitations we have are the ones we construct for ourselves.

Nowadays the standard in musicals is so high. There is no divide between the West End and provincial tours. The show has to be as good in Manchester or Edinburgh as it is in the West End. Playing a different town each week keeps you fresh. You have to convince each town, each audience, each set of critics that you're the best thing to come into their town for at least a week.

Critics are a necessary part of performing and producing and you have to live with them. The worst thing about reviews is that you only remember the really bad ones. When I'm in a show I don't allow reviews to be put up, good or bad. If the cast are interested enough, they can go to the company manager and ask to see them. It seems to me that you can't have one without the other and a negative review is not terrific for morale.

It's important to enjoy taking part in a show. I'm not saying that you should ad-lib or fool around. That can be irritating for an audience, it makes them feel excluded. The audience need to share the enjoyment of the show with you. I have more fun doing shows than anything else I do in my life, that's what makes me tick. For me, the fun and enjoyment of life comes through work, it's my biggest kick and when I feel most happy and relaxed.

I was very lucky that my mum took me as a boy of eight to see *Singin' in the Rain* because when I saw the magic of Gene Kelly, I knew then what I wanted to be.

I recently met my old record producer, Christopher Neil. We hadn't seen each other for twenty years. I was delighted to visit his home and see the many gold records he's received for his recordings of Celine Dion, Cher and Mike and The Mechanics to name but three. It's wonderful to see someone develop his or her talent and achieve great success.

I expect the same for David Ian, in the theatrical world. David is a natural producer and has the wonderful ability to make everybody feel comfortable. *Saturday Night Fever* was a difficult time for David, Robert and myself and at the end of it David decided – quite rightly – that he wanted to go out on his own. It was inevitable, David is a young guy and has to do his own thing. Of course we were both a little sad but we had a great seven years together and both learned a lot. We're the only producers I know who kiss each other at the beginning of a meeting. It always confused the opposition.

We still retain our company and have recently become involved with Paul 'The Commander' Elliot, Nick Thomas and John Conway, who put together a brand new musical of *Happy Days* based on the long-running American sitcom. I also had the great pleasure of meeting Henry Winkler – the original Fonz – who kindly came over to promote the British leg of the show. It opened in September 1999 in Australia as an Arena Production starring Craig McLachlan as the Fonz and Tom Boswell, who played the original Howard. Thereafter, we are hopeful of a large American production. Talk about taking coals to Newcastle. Or as the Fonz would say 'Perfectamundo! Aaay!'

Sadly, in the summer of 1999 Screaming Lord Sutch took his own life. I will always be grateful to Lord Sutch for opening my eyes to the possible. You meet very few one-offs in life, he was one. David Edward Sutch was unique.

Saturday Night Fever continues with great success at the London Palladium and productions in Germany and on Broadway are running with an Australian production commencing in February 2000.

Grease, a show that I have a special fondness for, closed in the West End in September 1999 whilst in its seventh year. The touring production continues to delight audiences around the country.

Robert Stigwood is as busy as ever and there's talk of us working together in the year 2000 on a new show.

My mum, now 80, lives in the coach house at the bottom of our garden surrounded by her family and has never been happier. The kids continue to flourish and seem a pretty well balanced bunch considering their gene pool. The grandchildren continue to call me Grandad but they'll learn. My darling Linzi never fails to amaze me by doing fifteen things simultaneously, while still helping me spell any word with more than four letters in it. Thanx.

As for me? I've been very lucky. My life has been a wonderful roller-coaster ride through the entertainment world. There have been highs and lows and occasionally, some stomach churning moments. It's always been fast and thrilling because I've never been sure what's waiting round the next bend.

So if you ask me what I want to do now, I'd have to say, 'I'd like another ride, please. Yeah, let's go round again.'

Index